**New Directions for
Institutional Research**

Paul D. Umbach
EDITOR-IN-CHIEF

J. Fredericks Volkwein
ASSOCIATE EDITOR

W9-BDS-437

Refining the Focus on Faculty Diversity in Postsecondary Institutions

Yonghong Jade Xu
EDITOR

Number 155 • Fall 2012
Jossey-Bass
San Francisco

REFINING THE FOCUS ON FACULTY DIVERSITY IN POSTSECONDARY
INSTITUTIONS
Yonghong Jade Xu (ed.)
New Directions for Institutional Research, no. 155
Paul D. Umbach, Editor-in-Chief

NEW DIRECTIONS FOR INSTITUTIONAL RESEARCH (ISSN 0271-0579, electronic
ISSN 1536-075X) is part of The Jossey-Bass Higher and Adult Education
Series and is published quarterly by Wiley Subscription Services, Inc., A
Wiley Company, at Jossey-Bass, One Montgomery Street, Suite 1200, San
Francisco, California 94104-4594 (publication number USPS 098-830).
Periodicals Postage Paid at San Francisco, California, and at additional
mailing offices. POSTMASTER: Send address changes to New Directions
for Institutional Research, Jossey-Bass, One Montgomery Street, Suite
1200, San Francisco, California 94104-4594.

INDIVIDUAL SUBSCRIPTION RATE (in USD): $89 per year US/Can/Mex, $113
rest of world; institutional subscription rate: $297 US, $337 Can/Mex, $371
rest of world. Single copy rate: $29. Electronic only–all regions: $89
individual, $297 institutional; Print & Electronic–US: $98 individual,
$342 institutional; Print & Electronic–Canada/Mexico: $98 individual,
$382 institutional; Print & Electronic–Rest of World: $122 individual, $416
institutional.

EDITORIAL CORRESPONDENCE should be sent to Paul D. Umbach, Leadership, Policy and Adult and Higher Education, North Carolina State University, Poe 300, Box 7801, Raleigh, NC 27695-7801.

New Directions for Institutional Research is indexed in *Academic Search*
(EBSCO), *Academic Search Elite* (EBSCO), *Academic Search Premier*
(EBSCO), *CIJE: Current Index to Journals in Education* (ERIC), *Contents
Pages in Education* (T&F), *EBSCO Professional Development Collection*
(EBSCO), *Educational Research Abstracts Online* (T&F), *ERIC Database*
(Education Resources Information Center), *Higher Education Abstracts*
(Claremont Graduate University), *Multicultural Education Abstracts*
(T&F), *Sociology of Education Abstracts* (T&F).

Microfilm copies of issues and chapters are available in 16mm and 35mm,
as well as microfiche in 105mm, through University Microfilms, Inc., 300
North Zeeb Road, Ann Arbor, Michigan 48106-1346.

www.josseybass.com

CONTENTS

EDITOR'S NOTES

Scholarly inquiry on the professional life of postsecondary faculty has always been a component of higher education research. During the past few decades, a variety of topics, including gender inequity, productivity, job satisfaction, and turnover have been studied extensively and their impact on the student outcomes well documented. In comparison, the primary "official" interest in postsecondary faculty by institutional researchers (IR) remains focused on salary studies and related gender/racial inequities. Expanding IR's limited focus appears necessary given the progressing diversity in faculty population and with the increasing confirmation of the value of diversity in enhancing the quality of higher education.

This volume includes chapters that examine faculty diversity from a variety of perspectives. The information provides institutional researchers with a comprehensive outlook on faculty diversity defined by factors including racial background, gender, citizenship, employment status, and academic discipline. Special attention is given to international faculty members and non-tenure-track faculty members, both groups having experienced rapid growth in recent years. Chapter authors present empirical evidence to argue that institutional research on faculty needs to be refined toward the increasing diversity in faculty population and actively tracking the changes over time, and to remain sensitive to the critical role of research methodology in effectively understanding how such increasing diversity has affected the work experience and productivity of faculty and the learning outcomes of students.

In Chapter One, Daryl G. Smith, Esau Tovar, and Hugo A. García present detailed and informative descriptive statistics on the postsecondary faculty population in the United States. Disaggregating the Integrated Postsecondary Education Data System (IPEDS) data by race/ethnicity, gender, and citizenship, and examining the distribution of full-time faculty across eleven institutional types, they assess the current state of full-time faculty diversity through: (1) the distribution of full-time faculty diversity within each institutional type; (2) the institutional distribution of faculty by each racial/gender grouping; and (3) the change over time between 1993 and 2009. What makes this chapter unique is the attention to historically black colleges and universities, tribal colleges, faculty in the for-profit sector, and international faculty. This chapter enables institutional researchers to evaluate the faculty diversity of their own institution within the context of the progressing diversity of U.S. faculty.

NEW DIRECTIONS FOR INSTITUTIONAL RESEARCH, no. 155, Fall 2012 © Wiley Periodicals, Inc.
Published online in Wiley Online Library (wileyonlinelibrary.com) • DOI: 10.1002/ir.20018

Attention is focused on international faculty in Chapter Two. Dong-bin Kim, Susan Twombly, and Lisa Wolf-Wendel use multiple data sources to illustrate the rapidly growing number of international faculty members at U.S. universities, in particular in the science, technology, engineering, and mathematics (STEM) fields. Further, the professional experience of international faculty members is examined in terms of their perception of academic life, productivity, and career mobility and compared with their U.S. faculty counterparts. By offering a better understanding of international faculty's experience, the authors discuss implications from the perspectives of academic labor market and the pipeline of new scholars.

In Chapter Three, Adrianna Kezar and Daniel Maxey offer another viewpoint on faculty diversity by highlighting the important role that non-tenure-track faculty (NTTF) play in the U.S. higher education system. Although NTTF are growing to be the majority of higher education faculty, they are largely misunderstood by their institutions and by the higher education community. The authors argue that one of the primary reasons that contributes to this problem is the lack of reliable data, including little or no data via IR offices about their hiring, numbers, and policies; departments' failure to send information to central HR/IR offices; and no qualitative data on NTTFs and the experiences and problems they face in creating a quality learning environment for students. The authors briefly review the national efforts by NTTFs to collect data on themselves, and they call upon institutional researchers for better data collection on this new faculty majority and also better models for understanding its implications.

Chapters Four and Five are included to demonstrate the methodological variations available to institutional researchers in their effort to document and understand faculty issues of growing complexity and diversity. Using Bayesian Network analysis, a nonparametric statistical procedure for modeling large-scale quantitative data, I analyzed data of three National Study of Postsecondary Faculty (NSOPF, 1993, 1999, and 2004) surveys in an effort to explore and compare the work experiences of women faculty in fields of different gender compositions, and to identify from a long-term perspective the factors that may negatively affect women in their low-presence areas. In Chapter Five, Vicente M. Lechuga employed a qualitative approach to offer an understanding of the role that emotions played in the academic work life of fifteen underrepresented faculty members in STEM disciplines, using an emotion management framework as a conceptual foundation. Interviews were conducted to collect qualitative data on participants' emotion management skills, and the author demonstrated how the manner in which emotions are managed has implications on faculty motivation.

In the final chapter, I synthesize the previous five chapters and offer a discussion on effective and efficient research strategies on university faculty from the perspectives of (1) being sensitive to subgroup differences among faculty population of an increasing diversity (in particular when studying the underrepresented groups), (2) actively tracking progress over time or including time as a dimension in order to understand the changes in the professional life of faculty, (3) the importance of rigorous data collection on faculty population, and (4) having flexibility in terms of choosing the appropriate methodology. Recommendations are provided for the practice of institutional researchers and for future research on university faculty.

Although student issues dominate institutional research, I hope to use this volume as an opportunity to argue that increased IR effort is needed to accurately profile and understand the needs of faculty through regular data collection and well-thought-out analyses. Faculty members are the primary production force of postsecondary institutions and have direct impact on student outcomes. As research has shown, diversification of faculty population on campus contributes to a greater range of ideas and perspectives, more minority role models, enriched curricula, better student academic performance, greater student satisfaction with their educational experience, a great cultural awareness, and a deeper appreciation of equity. With diversity gaining unprecedented emphasis as part of the institutional mission of colleges and universities, institutional researchers are expected to assume greater responsibilities in promoting research on faculty diversity. IR data collection and analyses play a critical role in assisting administrators and policymakers to obtain a better understanding of the serious implications of faculty performance, motivation, satisfaction, and professional well-being for the quality of higher education institutions. Additionally, tracking changes in the makeup of faculty population over time can provide guidance for strategic administrative actions in the process of increasing faculty diversity.

I would like to thank all the authors who contributed to this volume and the editor-in-chief, Paul Umbach, who provided me valuable advice on selecting topics and editing chapters.

Yonghong Jade Xu
Editor

YONGHONG JADE XU is an associate professor of educational research at the University of Memphis.

NEW DIRECTIONS FOR INSTITUTIONAL RESEARCH • DOI: 10.1002/ir

1

This introduction chapter presents descriptive statistics on the postsecondary faculty population in the United States and highlights the progressing diversity and growing number of minority, women, and international faculty.

Where Are They? A Multilens Examination of the Distribution of Full-Time Faculty by Institutional Type, Race/Ethnicity, Gender, and Citizenship

Daryl G. Smith, Esau Tovar, Hugo A. García

A rich body of literature has tracked and discussed faculty diversity with respect to race/ethnicity and gender for some time. This literature frequently looks at faculty diversity at the national level, or within a particular institution or sector. Extant literature often makes assumptions about the distribution of faculty of color at various institutions, suggesting, for example, that most Latino[1] faculty, like students, are at the community college (Contreras, 1998; Slaughter, 2007). For an up-to-date understanding, a more comprehensive, current, and in-depth analysis of faculty diversity focusing on race/ethnicity, gender and citizenship, and institutional type is needed.

Thus, this study provides a multilens examination of the diversity of full-time faculty in the United States across eleven institutional types derived from Carnegie classifications, by the intersection of race/ethnicity, citizenship, and gender and to make comparisons across time. Whereas few other studies have assessed faculty diversity for the for-profit sector (Schuster and Finkelstein, 2006), this study places emphasis on this rapidly growing type, along with the specific inclusion of historically black colleges and universities (HBCUs) and tribal colleges. In addition, the separation of international faculty from traditional race and ethnic categories

NEW DIRECTIONS FOR INSTITUTIONAL RESEARCH, no. 155, Fall 2012 © Wiley Periodicals, Inc.
Published online in Wiley Online Library (wileyonlinelibrary.com) • DOI: 10.1002/ir.20019

also provides an insight into that category and its impact on faculty diversity. The multilens perspective was made possible using three different analyses. Through the first lens, the distribution of full-time faculty diversity is examined *within each institutional type* (by gender, race/ethnicity, and citizenship). Through the second lens, there is an examination of the institutional distribution of faculty *within each racial-ethnic/gender grouping*. Finally, the third lens looks at *changes over time* and rates of change in faculty diversity by each of these categories from 1993 to 2009.

Literature Review

Research on the diversity of the American faculty across higher education segments continues to propagate (Turner, Gonzalez, and Wood, 2008). However, much of this research has relied on sample-based data sets (for example, National Study of Postsecondary Faculty [NSOPF]) to estimate faculty demographic characteristics, or was done some time ago, or has focused on particular institutions (see, for example, Antonio, 2002; Perna, 2003; Schuster and Finkelstein, 2006). In most instances, research by institutional type has focused on a limited range of institutional categories (for example, two-year/four-year, research/comprehensive/baccalaureate, or public/private to some degree), rather than on the comprehensiveness that characterizes institutional types across the country (Perna, 2003; Twombly, 1993; Wolf-Wendel, Ward, and Twombly, 2007). Additionally, much of this literature continues to focus on the experiences of faculty as a whole, with lesser attention paid to the status of individual racial/ethnic minority groups and of female faculty across institutional sectors (Perna, Gerald, Baum, and Milem, 2007; Townsend, 1995), or by the intersectionality of institutional type with gender and race/ethnicity (Perna, 2003; Smith, Altbach, and Lomotey, 2002). There seems to be a prevailing assumption that historically underrepresented faculty of color, especially blacks, Latinos, and American Indians, are found overwhelmingly at community colleges and at HBCUs (Alex-Assensoh, 2003; Allen and others, 2002; Contreras, 1998; Slaughter, 2007).

While the composition of the faculty has slowly become more diverse, Trower and Chait (2002) asserted that colleges and universities have done "too little for too long" (p. 34) to effect a significant change in faculty diversity. Similarly, Milem and Astin (1993) noted how little the composition of the faculty changed between 1972 and 1989, the years encompassing their study. Contrasting these views, Schuster and Finkelstein noted that a "pronounced escalation" in the diversification of faculty occurred between 1969 and 1998 (2006, p. 64). They reported that the overall percentage of full-time ethnic minority faculty at all institutions increased to 14.5 percent, and to 19.8 percent among new entrants. However, these gains were not equal for all racial/ethnic groups. Asians saw their numbers quadruple during the same period, followed by the tripling for blacks and Latinos, while the proportion of American Indians remained nearly identical to 1969 figures. However, none of these studies separated international faculty (noncitizens). Recent research suggests that, in fact, much of the growth in Asian faculty, in particular, and in Latino faculty, to some extent, is a function of growth in international faculty—"nonresident aliens" (NRAs) (Smith, 2009). Indeed, a recent study found that the racial distribution of ethnic faculty among international faculty was 30.5 percent Asian, 9.7 percent Latino, and 3.7 percent black (Mamiseishvili and Rosser, 2011).

In one of the few studies examining differences in the racial, ethnic, and gender composition of the faculty across institutional type, Milem and Astin (1993) found little evidence that the faculty had become more diverse. Using the 1972 American Council on Education and the 1989 Higher Education Research Institute's faculty surveys, weighted estimates were calculated to represent faculty at colleges and universities across the country. According to their estimates, faculty of color comprised 5 percent across all institutions in 1972 and 9.1 percent in 1989, nearly two decades later. The authors reported that in 1972, the largest proportion of faculty of color were at public four-year institutions (7.8 percent), whereas the lowest were at private four-year colleges (3.7 percent). By 1989, faculty of color were the least represented at private four-year colleges (6.7 percent), while public two-year colleges achieved the greatest representation (10.6 percent). The most significant change found in the same period by racial/ethnic group was the more than doubling of Asian faculty across all types (1.3 percent to 2.9 percent). But more striking was their tripling at public universities (1.4 percent to 4.1 percent). With a slight increase in the percentage of black faculty overall (1.3 percent to 2.1 percent), they remained the least represented at public universities (0.7 percent) and best represented at public two-year colleges (3.3 percent). By contrast, the percentage of Latino and American Indian faculty remained largely unchanged at less than 1 percent at all institutions, save for the 2 percent represented by Latinos at two-year colleges. Finally, with respect to the advancement of women, Milem and Astin (1993) cited a seven-percentage-point gain in the same period across all institutional types (21.4 percent versus 28.3 percent), but their gains are the least at private universities and the greatest at public two-year colleges.

Schuster and Finkelstein (2006) also examined faculty diversity by institutional type. They reported that the diversification of the American faculty has progressed "steadily" regardless of the institutional type examined. Using data from four faculty surveys (Carnegie Commission National Survey of Faculty and Student Opinion 1969; NSOPF 1988, 1993, and 1999), the authors noted that faculty of color across all institutional types comprised 3.8 percent in 1969, 10.7 percent in 1987, 13.3 percent in 1988, and increased to 14.5 percent by 1992. Schuster and Finkelstein took particular notice of the representation that has been achieved by ethnic minority faculty at universities where they made up 14.7 percent in 1992, the last full year they reported for all faculty. They constituted 14.2 percent at "other" four-year institutions and 14.3 percent at two-year colleges in the same year.

Similarly, Perna (2001, 2003) has looked at the racial profile of faculty comparing two- and four-year institutions using NSOPF 1993 data. Again, looking at institutional profiles, she found that traditionally underrepresented ethnic minority faculty were less present at four-year institutions as compared to two-year colleges in 1992. The corresponding percentages reported were 5.1 percent versus 5.5 percent for African Americans, 2.3 percent versus 4.6 percent for Latinos, and 0.3 percent versus 0.9 percent for American Indians, respectively. However, she noted that minorities are slightly better represented at the lower levels of faculty ranks and experience. Of significance to this current study is the finding that Latinos and American Indians, compared to whites and Asians, were more likely to be employed at public community colleges than at four-year colleges. With respect to women, Perna (2001) found that women were underrepresented at research universities, while overrepresented at comprehensive universities, even when controlling for rank and experience.

With respect to community colleges, research suggests that faculty of color and white women have made significant progress in gaining access to the faculty ranks (Gahn and Twombly, 2001; Milem and Astin, 1993; Perna, 2003). But the argument has also been made that they have been relegated to teach at these "less prestigious" institutions (Seidman, 1985; Snyder, Dillow, and Hoffman, 2009; Townsend, 1995, 1998). Given these statistics, some authors have suggested that women, particularly those from ethnic minorities, are now vastly overrepresented at two-year institutions as compared to four-year institutions (Antonio, 2002; Bower, 2002; Perna, 2003; Schuster and Finkelstein, 2006).

While many researchers seem to support the assumption that historically underrepresented faculty would be located more frequently in community colleges, we found no recent study that provides the in-depth analysis on the current diversity of faculty in the United States, examining the intersectionality of institutional type, race/ethnicity, gender, and citizenship. Consistently engaging in evaluations and research studies that monitor progress globally across institutions and across broad faculty groupings does little in portraying the true state of affairs for faculty diversity across institutional types, race/ethnicity, gender, and citizenship. Hence, this study examines the representation of full-time faculty across eleven institutional types derived from Carnegie classifications, by racial/ethnic group (including international faculty), by gender, and across time. This chapter specifically addresses the following questions:

- What is the overall current landscape of full-time faculty diversity in the United States across institutional types: by gender, race/ethnicity, and citizenship?

- Where are faculty from different race/ethnicity, gender, and citizenship groups located across institutional types?
- How did these patterns change from 1993 to 2009?

Method

Data Sources. This study provides a descriptive analysis of the diversity of the postsecondary full-time faculty at degree-granting institutions in the United States and details the changes that took place between 1993 and 2009 with respect to diversity by gender, race/ethnicity, and citizenship across eleven institutional types. The study uses population data reported by individual institutions through the Integrated Postsecondary Education Data System (IPEDS) sponsored by the National Center for Education Statistics (NCES). A custom file containing institution-level data for all variables of interest was downloaded directly from the IPEDS Data Center. The years examined were limited to 1993 and 2009; 1993 was the first year when NCES collected data for "nonresident alien" (NRA) faculty as a separate "racial/ethnic" group.

Institutional Types. For the purpose of this study, institutions in U.S. territories, such as Puerto Rico and Guam, were excluded. While the current basic Carnegie classification system includes thirty-three institutional types, we reduced these by combining similar types.[2] For example, the ten public associate degree categories were combined into one to better manage data analysis. The same scheme was followed for the remaining Carnegie classifications. Accordingly, as shown in Table 1.1, for the year 2009, 4,055 institutions met our criteria for inclusion in the study. The public sector included 1,031 two-year colleges, 168 research universities, 261 master's-level universities, and 136 baccalaureate institutions. The private not-for-profit (NFP) sector included 94 two-year colleges, 105 research universities, and 843 master's/baccalaureate institutions, while the private for-profit sector spanned 550 two-year and 125 four-year colleges. Finally, the special focus category included 31 tribal colleges, 711 "other" special focus institutions, and 96 HBCUs. In 1993, 3,088 institutions were included with distributions that closely mirrored the 2009 data. Special focus institutions include those that award at least a baccalaureate degree, with a high concentration of these in a single field or set of related fields (for example, seminaries, schools of law). The designation for HBCUs is provided in our data tables and discussed in the chapter for illustrative purposes, but these institutions are all accounted for among the other institutional types.

Race/Ethnicity and Citizenship. The racial and ethnic categories used align with the reporting categories for IPEDS: African American, Latino, American Indian/Alaska Native (AI/AN), Asian American/Pacific Islander (AA/PI), and white. Since 1993, international faculty of all racial groups—"nonresident aliens (NRAs)"—have been placed in a separate category. This allows us to study faculty diversity from a domestic perspective.

NEW DIRECTIONS FOR INSTITUTIONAL RESEARCH • DOI: 10.1002/ir

Table 1.1. Distribution of Institutional Type and Full-Time Faculty at Title IV Degree-Granting Institutions in the Fifty United States: Fall 1993 and 2009

Institutional Type	Distribution of Institutions Selected				Distribution of Full-Time Faculty			
	1993		2009		1993		2009	
	n	Pct.	n	Pct.	n	Pct.	n	Pct.
Public								
Two-year	894	29.0	1031	25.4	91506	28.9	119750	16.7
Research	165	5.3	168	4.1	173789	5.4	224823	31.3
Master's	260	8.4	261	6.4	75506	8.4	90544	12.6
Baccalaureate	126	4.1	136	3.4	11954	4.1	16029	2.2
Private NFP								
Two-year	55	1.8	94	2.3	1181	1.8	1768	0.2
Research	104	3.4	105	2.6	66172	3.4	108821	15.1
MA/BA	802	26.0	843	20.8	69365	26.1	92666	12.9
Private For-Profit								
Two-year FP	114	3.7	550	13.6	1754	3.7	10246	1.4
Four-year FP	47	1.5	125	3.1	1332	1.4	4024	0.6
Special Purpose								
Tribal colleges	20	0.6	31	0.8	560	0.6	761	0.1
Other—special focus	502	16.2	711	17.5	35282	16.3	49095	6.8
Total	3088	100	4055	100	528371	100	718527	100
HBCU[a]	94	3	96	2.4	13242	2.5	15654	2.2

[a]The HBCUs classification is provided for illustration purposes only; institutions and faculty are all part of the other categories.

Results

Table 1.1 provides an overview of the distribution of institutional types and corresponding percentages of full-time faculty. In 2009, there were a total of 718,527 faculty members in higher education within the fifty states. Almost half of all faculty (46.3 percent) were in public and private research institutions, 18.3 percent in two-year (virtually all public), and 27.7 percent in BA- and MA-granting institutions. This accounts for 92.4 percent of all full-time faculty. Though two-year public institutions were 25.4 percent of all institutions in the United States, they employed only 16.7 percent of the full-time faculty. In contrast, while public and private research institutions constitute only 6.7 percent of all institutions, they employed nearly half (46.4 percent) of the full-time faculty. Although the for-profit sector is growing fast and constitutes 16.7 percent of all institutions, it represented just 2.0 percent of all full-time faculty. HBCUs

NEW DIRECTIONS FOR INSTITUTIONAL RESEARCH • DOI: 10.1002/ir

Figure 1.1. Fall 2009 Distribution of Full-Time Faculty Within Institutional Type by Race/Ethnicity and Citizenship

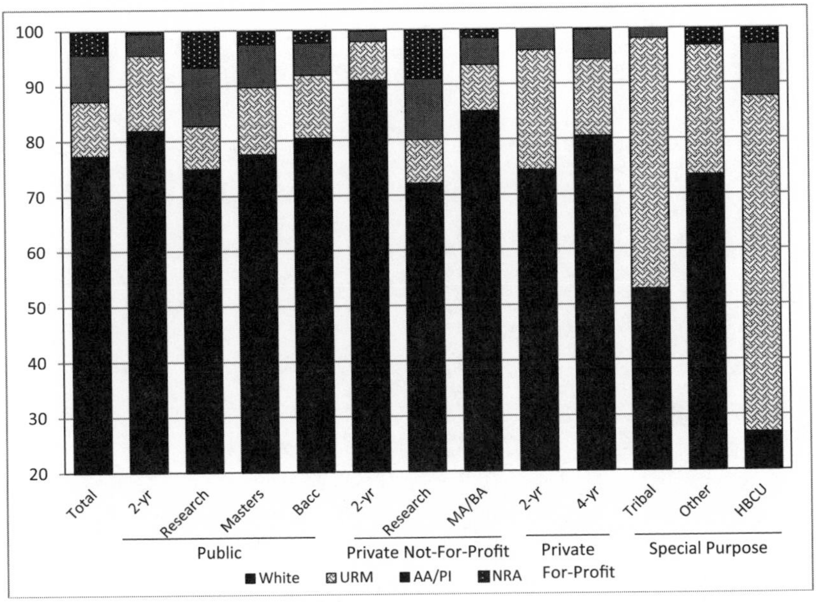

AI/AN = American Indian/Alaska Native; AA/PI = Asian American/Pacific Islander.

employed 2.2 percent of all faculty and accounted for 2.4 percent of all institutions.

Table 1.2 shows the race and gender distribution for the faculty as a whole (with the "unknown faculty" removed) as of fall 2009. This table should be read horizontally to see the distribution of faculty by race *within* institutional type. Overall, 58 percent of the faculty were male, and there were more men than women within each racial group with the exception of black faculty. White faculty represented 77.3 percent of all faculty (44.2 percent male, 33.2 percent female), black faculty were 5.5 percent (2.5 percent male, 3.0 percent female), Latino faculty were 3.9 percent of all faculty (2.1 percent male, 1.8 percent female), and AI/AN faculty were 0.5 percent (equally male and female). Thus, in 2009, historically underrepresented faculty (black, Latino, AI/AN) were 9.9 percent of all full-time faculty. AA/PI faculty represented 8.5 percent of all full-time faculty in 2009 (5.3 percent male, 3.2 percent female), and international faculty of all race/ethnicities (NRA) were 4.4 percent (2.9 percent male, 1.5 percent female).

Faculty Diversity by Institutional Type. Table 1.2 also provides the data to understand the diversity of faculty by race and gender within each institutional type. Whether the public two-year institutions are more diverse, as generally reflected in the literature, can be examined through this lens. In looking at the racial distribution, Figure 1.1 provides a

Table 1.2. Percentage of Full-Time Faculty by Race/Ethnicity, Gender, Citizenship Within Institutional Type: Fall 2009 (Unknown Excluded)

Institutional Type	All Races		White			Black		
	Total	% F	M	F	T	M	F	T
Public								
Two-year	117723	54.0	38	43.9	81.9	2.8	4.4	7.2
Research	220104	37.9	46.3	28.6	74.9	2	2	4
Master's	88976	45.5	42	35.5	77.5	3.6	3.9	7.5
Baccalaureate	15569	43.8	45.3	35	80.4	3.9	4.1	8
Private NFP								
Two-year	1756	55.0	40.8	50	90.8	2.2	2.8	5
Research	106273	36.3	46.6	25.5	72.1	2	2.2	4.2
MA/BA	90836	45.2	47.1	37.9	85.1	2.6	2.9	5.5
Private For-Profit								
Two-year	9858	52.6	36	38.3	74.4	4.8	8.6	13.4
Four-year	3822	47.8	42.5	37.9	80.5	3.9	5.6	9.5
Special Purpose								
Tribal colleges	756	50.1	25.4	27.4	52.8	0.7	0.3	0.9
Other—special focus	48443	40.2	44.4	29	73.4	2.4	2.7	5.1
Total %	100	42.9	44.2	33.2	77.3	2.5	3	5.5
N	704116		311074	233482	544556	17734	21164	38898
HBCU[a]	15266	45.8	15.8	11	26.8	28	30.2	58.2

Note: In fall 2009 there were 8,148 male and 6,263 female unknown faculty in terms of race/ethnicity.
[a]The HBCU classification is provided for illustration purposes only; faculty at these institutions are all tabulated in the other categories.

summary of the findings in Table 1.2, with particular attention to four broad race and citizenship categories: white; underrepresented minority (URM: black, Latino, AI/AN); AA/PI; and NRA. Looking at the percentage of URM faculty in the public sector, two-year institutions had the highest percentage of URM (13.6 percent), and research universities the lowest (7.8 percent). However, the variation among these sectors is not as great as the literature has suggested (for example, Slaughter, 2007). Indeed, baccalaureate institutions had 11.4 percent URM, master's 12.2 percent. In the private NFP sector, a different pattern emerges. The two-year private institutions, a relatively tiny portion of all institutions, had the lowest percentage of URM faculty (7.0 percent), and there was no difference in the percentage of URM faculty between research universities and BA/MA institutions, with both sectors having about 8 percent.

Significantly, as noted in Table 1.2, the proprietary sector employed the highest percentages of URM faculty (except for the tribal colleges and HBCUs), though overall they are quite a small sector. Tribal colleges employed 43 percent American Indian faculty, and HBCUs employed 58 percent black faculty.

Thus, while one might conclude that two-year institutions are more diverse with respect to URM faculty, the differences are fairly small. From the perspective of the percentage of white faculty or the percentage of NRA faculty, another picture emerges. The percentage of white faculty

Table 1.2. Percentage of Full-Time Faculty by Race/Ethnicity, Gender, Citizenship Within Institutional Type: Fall 2009 (Continued)

	Latino			AA/PI			AI/AN			NRA	
M	F	T	M	F	T	M	F	T	M	F	T
2.7	3	5.7	1.8	2.1	3.9	0.3	0.3	0.7	0.3	0.3	0.6
1.9	1.5	3.4	7.2	3.4	10.6	0.2	0.2	0.4	4.5	2.1	6.7
2.1	1.9	4.1	4.9	2.8	7.7	0.3	0.3	0.6	1.6	1	2.6
1.6	1.3	2.9	3.6	2.2	5.8	0.2	0.3	0.5	1.5	0.9	2.4
1	0.7	1.8	0.7	1.2	1.9	0.1	0.1	0.2	0.2	0.1	0.3
2	1.5	3.5	6.8	4.1	11	0.1	0.1	0.2	6.1	3	9
1.4	1.4	2.8	2.6	2.1	4.8	0.1	0.1	0.3	0.9	0.7	1.7
4.2	3.7	7.8	2.1	1.8	3.9	0.3	0.2	0.5	0	0	0
1.6	1.9	3.6	3.3	2	5.4	0.5	0.3	0.8	0.2	0.1	0.3
1.2	0.8	2	1.1	0.8	1.9	21.6	20.9	42.5	0	0	0
2.3	1.7	4	8.6	5.7	14.3	0.1	0.1	0.3	1.9	1	2.9
2.1	1.8	3.9	5.3	3.2	8.4	0.2	0.2	0.5	2.9	1.5	4.4
14566	12835	27401	36973	22204	59177	1724	1695	3419	20201	10464	30665
1.2	1	2.2	6.9	2.6	9.4	0.2	0.1	0.3	2.2	0.8	3

AI/AN = American Indian/Alaska Native; AA/PI = Asian American/Pacific Islander.

was, indeed, among the highest at two-year public campuses (81.9 percent). This pattern is directly related to the percentage of NRA faculty. While NRA faculty are 6.7 percent and 9.0 percent of the faculty at public and private research universities, respectively, their representation is negligible in two-year institutions.

Information in Table 1.2 also shows a consistent pattern at the intersection of race and gender. Overall and within most institutional types, men constitute about 57 percent of the faculty. In the two-year sector, women are in the majority, 54 percent overall and for each racial group (or equal for American Indians and NRA faculty). The percentage of men is greatest at research universities, public and private, where they were 62 percent and 64 percent, respectively—a pattern that held for all ethnic groups except blacks and American Indians, where gender was more closely balanced. This pattern is true for the other four-year institutions as well, though the figures are less skewed. Within each institutional type, there is some diversity with respect to race, gender, and citizenship. However, with respect to URM faculty, the two-year institutions, while having more women, do not have dramatically more URM faculty.

Institutional Distribution Within Race and Gender Categories. Table 1.3 and Figure 1.2 show the overall distribution of faculty across institutional types within race and gender. Table 1.3 should be read vertically to see the distribution of faculty by race/ethnicity. Over

Table 1.3. Percentage of Full-Time Faculty Within Race/Ethnicity, Gender by Sector: Fall 2009 (Unknown Excluded)

Inst. Type		All Races Total	White			Black		
			M	F	T	M	F	T
Public								
Two-year	%	16.7	14.4	22.1	17.7	18.3	24.6	21.8
	N	117723	44732	51653	96385	3250	5216	8466
Research	%	31.3	32.8	27	30.3	24.3	21.1	22.6
	N	220104	101918	62941	164859	4309	4469	8778
Master's	%	12.6	12	13.5	12.7	18.2	16.5	17.3
	N	88976	37394	31550	68944	3219	3497	6716
Baccalaureate	%	2.2	2.3	2.3	2.3	3.5	3	3.2
	N	15569	7057	5453	12510	612	638	1250
Private NFP								
Two-year	%	0.2	0.2	0.4	0.3	0.2	0.2	0.2
	N	1756	716	878	1594	39	49	88
Research	%	15.1	15.9	11.6	14.1	12.3	10.9	11.5
	N	106273	49549	27055	76604	2178	2303	4481
MA/BA	%	12.9	13.8	14.8	14.2	13.2	12.4	12.8
	N	90836	42825	34454	77279	2342	2630	4972
Private For-Profit								
Two-year	%	1.4	1.1	1.6	1.3	2.7	4	3.4
	N	9858	3553	3777	7330	476	843	1319
Four-year	%	0.5	0.5	0.6	0.6	0.8	1	0.9
	N	3822	1626	1449	3075	150	213	363
Special purpose								
Tribal colleges	%	0.1	0.1	0.1	0.1	0	0	0.0
	N	756	192	207	399	5	2	7
Other— Special focus	%	6.9	6.9	6	6.5	6.5	6.2	6.3
	N	48443	21512	14065	35577	1154	1304	2458
Total	%	100	100	100	100	100	100	100
	N	704116	311074	233482	544556	17734	21164	38898
HBCU[a]	%	2.2%	0.8%	0.7%	0.8	24.1	21.8	22.8
	N	15266	2410	1678	4088	4269	4617	8886

[a]Number and percentage of faculty at HBCU institutions are provided for illustrative purposes only.

one-third (34.1 percent) of black and two-fifths (41.1 percent) of Latino faculty are at research universities, 17.3 percent and 12.8 percent at public master's institutions, respectively, and nearly one-quarter are at community colleges (24.6 percent for blacks and 24.4 percent for Latinos). Among AI/AN faculty, 35 percent work at research universities, 23.8 percent in two-year publics (non-tribal), and 15.9 percent at public master's institutions. For AA/PI, the distribution looks quite different. Almost three of five (59.0 percent) are employed at research universities and another 11.6 percent in public master's institutions. While the percentage of Black and Latino faculty at all two-year institutions (about 24 percent) was higher than the overall distribution of faculty (17.3 percent), it is still true that the highest percentage of URM faculty were at research universities.

Table 1.3. Percentage of Full-Time Faculty Within Race/Ethnicity, Gender by Sector: Fall 2009 (Continued)

Latino			AA/PI			AI/AN			NRA		
M	F	T	M	F	T	M	F	T	M	F	T
22	27.1	24.4	5.8	11.2	7.8	23.5	23.8	23.7	2	3.4	2.5
3207	3483	6690	2128	2482	4610	405	404	809	403	360	763
29.3	25.5	27.5	42.7	33.7	39.3	27.6	30	28.8	49.3	45.1	47.9
4266	3269	7535	15786	7485	23271	476	508	984	9961	4716	14677
13	13.4	13.2	11.7	11.4	11.6	16.1	15.9	16.0	6.9	8.9	7.5
1895	1715	3610	4316	2528	6844	278	269	547	1388	927	2315
1.7	1.6	1.6	1.5	1.5	1.5	2.1	2.7	2.4	1.1	1.4	1.2
248	201	449	564	340	904	37	45	82	230	144	374
0.1	0.1	0.1	0	0.1	0.1	0.1	0.1	0.1	0	0	0.0
18	13	31	13	21	34	1	2	3	4	2	6
14.5	12.6	13.6	19.7	19.7	19.7	6.8	6	6.4	31.8	30.2	31.3
2105	1621	3726	7266	4384	11650	117	101	218	6430	3164	9594
8.5	9.9	9.1	6.4	8.8	7.3	7.2	6.7	6.9	4.2	6.3	4.9
1240	1266	2506	2382	1951	4333	124	113	237	851	658	1509
2.8	2.8	2.8	0.5	0.8	0.6	1.9	1.1	1.5	0	0	0.0
410	362	772	203	181	384	32	19	51	0	2	2
0.4	0.6	0.5	0.3	0.4	0.3	1.1	0.6	0.8	0	0	0.0
63	74	137	128	78	206	19	10	29	8	4	12
0.1	0	0.1	0	0	0.0	9.5	9.3	9.4	0	0	0.0
9	6	15	8	6	14	163	158	321	0	0	0
7.6	6.4	7.0	11.3	12.4	11.7	4.2	3.9	4.0	4.6	4.7	4.6
1105	825	1930	4179	2748	6927	72	66	138	926	487	1413
100	100	100	100	100	100	100	100	100	100	100	100
14566	12835	27401	36973	22204	59177	1724	1695	3419	20201	10464	30665
1.2	1.2	1.2	2.8	1.8	2.4	1.7	1.1	1.4	1.7	1.2	1.5
182	160	342	1048	392	1440	30	19	49	337	124	461

AI/AN = American Indian/Alaska Native; AA/PI = Asian American/Pacific Islander.

Indeed, of the 69,718 URM faculty, 46,091 or 66 percent were at public and private research and baccalaureate institutions.

When gender is taken into consideration, Table 1.4 shows higher percentages of black and Latina women at two-year colleges than other groups at 29 percent and 30 percent, respectively. However, over one-third are still at research universities. In addition, black and Latino men are found at research institutions at significantly higher percentages (37 percent and 44 percent) than at two-year institutions (21 percent and 25 percent). NRA men and women had the highest percentage of representation at research institutions at 81 percent and 75 percent and the lowest representation at two-year public institutions, at 2 percent and 3 percent, respectively.

Figure 1.2. Fall 2009 Distribution of Full-Time Faculty by Institutional Type Within Race/Ethnicity, Gender, and Citizenship

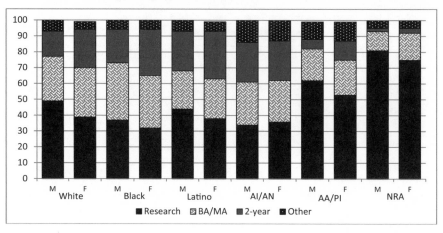

AI/AN = American Indian/Alaska Native; AA/PI = Asian American/Pacific Islander.

Table 1.4. Total Percentage of Faculty by Institutional Type Within Race/Ethnicity, Gender, and Citizenship: Fall 2009

Race/Gender	Research[a]	BA/MA	Two-year	Other[b]	Total
White					
Male	49	28	16	7	100
Female	39	31	24	5	100
Black					
Male	37	36	21	7	100
Female	32	33	29	6	100
Latino					
Male	44	24	25	8	100
Female	38	25	30	6	100
AI/AN					
Male	34	27	25	14	100
Female	36	26	25	13	100
AA/PI					
Male	62	20	6	11	100
Female	53	22	12	12	100
NRA					
Male	81	12	2	5	100
Female	75	17	3	5	100
Total					
Male	51	15	27	7	100
Female	40	30	23	7	100

[a]Public and Private, NFP combined.
[b]Includes Tribal Colleges.
Note: Totals may not add up to 100% due to rounding error.
AI/AN = American Indian/Alaska Native; AA/PI = Asian American/Pacific Islander.

Change Over Time. Table 1.1 and Table 1.5 show the changes in numbers of faculty between 1993 and 2009. The number of faculty at degree-granting institutions was 527,480 in 1993 (if unknowns were included, the faculty grew from 528,371 in 1993 to 718,527 or 36 percent). By 2009, faculty had grown to 704,116, representing a total growth of 33 percent across institutional types. As shown in Table 1.1, the distribution of faculty across institutional types differs between 1993 and 2009. In particular, while 29 percent of all faculty were in two-year institutions in 1993, only 17 percent were there in 2009. The research institutions, both public and private, grew to 45 percent of all faculty in 2009 from 9 percent in 1993. Most notably illustrated in Table 1.5 is the significant expansion of faculty at two- and four-year for-profit institutions, where faculty grew by 466 percent and 188 percent, respectively, while the lowest growth occurred at HBCUs (16 percent) and public master's (18 percent) institutions. Within two-year for-profit institutions, Latino faculty grew the fastest at an astonishing 2,044 percent, followed by African Americans at 1,303 percent—although given the barely visible presence of these faculty in 1993 in this subset, striking percentage increases would appear only increasing hires by modest amounts numerically.

Examining the raw numbers for race/ethnicity and gender, as illustrated in Table 1.5 and Figure 1.3, we find substantial differences in percentage growth between 1993 and 2009. Specifically, white faculty grew by 20 percent (with women growing 56 percent), blacks by 58 percent (women by 80 percent), Latinos by 132 percent (women by 185 percent), AA/PI by 140 percent (women by 260 percent), AI/AN by 85 percent (women by 131 percent), and NRAs by 188 percent (women by 333 percent). In addition, white males grew in number, though this group had the lowest percentage growth, at 2 percent among all groups. Figure 1.3 shows the growth in the percentage of women in each racial group from 1993 to 2009, as well as the changes by percentage by race in the faculty as a whole. It is worth noting that, despite the growth in numbers for each racial group and the relative decrease in the percentage of white faculty, there were relatively small changes in the racial makeup of the faculty overall in these two time periods.

Trends in Growth by Institutional Type. From 1993 to 2009, the overall racial patterns have remained largely the same, with a growth of one or two percentage points for faculty of color. Overall, URM faculty grew from 38,335 of 527,480 faculty (7.3 percent) to 69,718 of 704,116 (9.9 percent) in this sixteen-year period. Table 1.6 provides a summary of changes in racial diversity by institutional type. Overall, white faculty slipped from 86 percent to 77 percent of all faculty, while each of the other groups increased by a small amount. Black faculty grew from 5 percent to 6 percent, Latino faculty from 2 percent to 4 percent, AA/PI faculty from 5 percent to 8 percent, and NRA faculty from 2 percent to 4 percent.

There are a few instances where changes were somewhat larger. Table 1.6 provides a summary of the findings showing growth from 3 percent to

Table 1.5. Percent Change in Number of Full-Time Faculty by Race/ Ethnicity, Gender, Citizenship, and Institutional Type: 1993 and 2009 (Unknown Excluded)

Institutional Type	Percent Change	All Races	White			Black		
		Total	M	F	T	M	F	T
Public								
Two-year	% Change	29	0	45	20	44	61	54
	2009	117723	44732	51653	96385	3250	5216	8466
	1993	91422	44843	35732	80575	2264	3245	5509
Research	% Change	27	−5	55	11	33	70	50
	2009	220104	101918	62941	164859	4309	4469	8778
	1993	173516	107251	40716	147967	3232	2635	5867
Master's	% Change	18	−10	47	9	6	39	21
	2009	88976	37394	31550	68944	3219	3497	6716
	1993	75409	41709	21498	63207	3039	2514	5553
Baccalaureate	% Change	31	4	59	22	44	69	56
	2009	15569	7057	5453	12510	612	638	1250
	1993	11850	6810	3440	10250	424	377	801
Private NFP								
Two-year	% Change	50	33	53	43	333	227	267
	2009	1756	716	878	1594	39	49	88
	1993	1172	539	574	1113	9	15	24
Research	% Change	61	21	82	37	46	128	79
	2009	106273	49549	27055	76604	2178	2303	4481
	1993	66126	40989	14867	55856	1492	1012	2504
MA/BA	% Change	31	8	52	24	46	97	70
	2009	90836	42825	34454	77279	2342	2630	4972
	1993	69169	39775	22619	62394	1599	1334	2933
Private For-Profit								
Two-year	% Change	466	316	465	381	707	2309	1303
	2009	9858	3553	3777	7330	476	843	1319
	1993	1743	855	668	1523	59	35	94
Four-year	% Change	188	105	260	157	384	1320	689
	2009	3822	1626	1449	3075	150	213	363
	1993	1325	792	403	1195	31	15	46
Special Purpose								
Tribal colleges	% Change	35	−14	29	4	400	100	250
	2009	756	192	207	399	5	2	7
	1993	558	223	161	384	1	1	2
Other— special focus	% Change	38	7	53	21	53	122	83
	2009	48443	21512	14065	35577	1154	1304	2458
	1993	35190	20174	9175	29349	752	588	1340
All Types								
Total	% Change	33	2	56	20	37	80	58
	2009	704116	311074	233482	544556	17734	21164	38898
	1993	527480	303960	149853	453813	12902	11771	24673
HBCU[a]	% Change	16	−5	9	0	4	35	18
	2009	15266	2410	1678	4088	4269	4617	8886
	1993	13167	2534	1534	4068	4122	3415	7537

[a]The HBCU classification is provided for illustration purposes only; faculty at these institutions are all tabulated as part of the other categories.

NEW DIRECTIONS FOR INSTITUTIONAL RESEARCH • DOI: 10.1002/ir

Table 1.5. Percentage Change in Number of Full-Time Faculty by Race/Ethnicity, Gender, Citizenship, and Institutional Type: 1993 and 2009 (Continued)

Latino			AA/PI			AI/AN			NRA		
M	F	T	M	F	T	M	F	T	M	F	T
101	183	136	108	182	142	38	105	65	391	1025	569
3207	3483	6690	2128	2482	4610	405	404	809	403	360	763
1598	1232	2830	1025	879	1904	293	197	490	82	32	114
90	195	124	99	278	134	53	137	87	114	292	150
4266	3269	7535	15786	7485	23271	476	508	984	9961	4716	14677
2248	1110	3358	7950	1980	9930	311	214	525	4665	1204	5869
60	133	88	50	213	86	25	128	60	161	433	228
1895	1715	3610	4316	2528	6844	278	269	547	1388	927	2315
1185	735	1920	2875	807	3682	223	118	341	532	174	706
71	230	118	64	262	106	106	105	105	180	336	225
248	201	449	564	340	904	37	45	82	230	144	374
145	61	206	344	94	438	18	22	40	82	33	115
100	86	94	63	133	100		100	200	300		500
18	13	31	13	21	34	1	2	3	4	2	6
9	7	16	8	9	17	0	1	1	1	0	1
134	179	152	138	365	192	166	274	207	275	525	332
2105	1621	3726	7266	4384	11650	117	101	218	6430	3164	9594
901	580	1481	3053	942	3995	44	27	71	1713	506	2219
97	168	128	60	201	103	121	131	126	156	294	202
1240	1266	2506	2382	1951	4333	124	113	237	851	658	1509
628	472	1100	1489	648	2137	56	49	105	333	167	500
1950	2163	2044	577	2163	911	−24		21	−100	−67	−80
410	362	772	203	181	384	32	19	51	0	2	2
20	16	36	30	8	38	42	0	42	4	6	10
385	517	448	172	1460	296	533		867	300	100	200
63	74	137	128	78	206	19	10	29	8	4	12
13	12	25	47	5	52	3	0	3	2	2	4
800	500	650	100	200	133	104	90	97		−100	−100
9	6	15	8	6	14	163	158	321	0	0	0
1	1	2	4	2	6	80	83	163	0	1	1
96	196	129	151	243	180	71	200	116	11	67	26
1105	825	1930	4179	2748	6927	72	66	138	926	487	1413
564	279	843	1668	802	2470	42	22	64	833	291	1124
99	185	132	100	260	140	55	131	85	145	333	188
14566	12835	27401	36973	22204	59177	1724	1695	3419	20201	10464	30665
7312	4505	11817	18493	6176	24669	1112	733	1845	8247	2416	10663
90	171	121	5	97	21	67	217	104	104	396	143
182	160	342	1048	392	1440	30	19	49	337	124	461
96	59	155	994	199	1193	18	6	24	165	25	190

AI/AN = American Indian/Alaska Native; AA/PI = Asian American/Pacific Islander.

Figure 1.3. Full-Time Faculty Distribution by Race/Ethnicity and Gender: 1993 and 2009

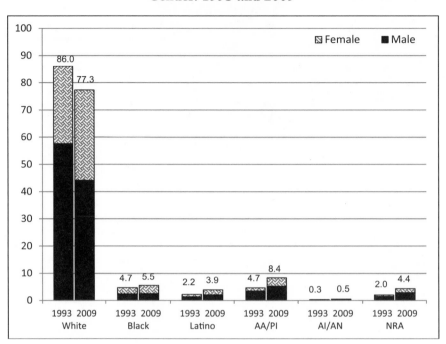

AI/AN = American Indian, Alaska Native; AA/PI = Asian American/ Pacific Islander.

6 percent for Latino faculty at public two-year institutions, and a six-percentage-point growth in NRA faculty at private NFP research institutions. The percentage of AI/AN faculty at tribal colleges grew from 29 percent to 43 percent. The proprietary sector also shows significant growth in black and Latino faculty, doubling and tripling their representation in both two- and four-year institutions.

Furthermore, data in Tables 1.5 and 1.6 indicate that white males and AI/AN men were the only groups to decrease in percentage at some sectors of higher education. For example, white men decreased as a percentage from 1993 to 2009 at public research (−5 percent), master's and public master's (−10 percent). Among special focus institutions males dropped 14 percent, and in the case of HBCUs, white males decreased 5 percent. Although the faculty grew significantly at two-year proprietary institutions, AI/AN men decreased 24 percent at private for-profit two-year institutions. In addition to AI/AN men, NRA men and women decreased in number from 4 percent and 6 percent, respectively, to zero and 2 percent, respectively, within these institutions in 2009.

Changes in Distribution of Faculty by Race and Gender Over Time. The race and gender patterns seen for the distribution of faculty in 2009

Table 1.6. Full-Time Faculty by Race/Ethnicity and Citizenship Within Institutional Type: 1993 and 2009 by Percent

	White		Black		Latino		AA/PI		AI/AN		NRA	
Year (1993/2009)	93	09	93	09	93	09	93	09	93	09	93	09
Institutional Type												
Public												
Two-year	88	82	6	7	3	6	2	4	0.5	0.7	0.1	0.6
Research	85	75	3	4	2	3	6	11	0.3	0.4	3	7
Master's	84	77	7	8	3	4	5	8	0.5	0.6	0.9	3
Baccalaureate	86	80	7	8	2	3	4	6	0.3	0.5	1	2
Private NFP												
Two-year	95	91	2	5	1	2	1	2	0.0	0.2	0.0	0.3
Research	84	72	4	4	2	4	6	11	0.1	0.2	3	9
MA/BA	90	85	4	6	2	3	3	5	0.2	0.3	0.7	2
Private For-Profit												
Two-year	87	74	5	13	2	8	2	4	0.2	0.5	0.6	0.0
Four-year	90	80	3	10	2	4	4	5	0.2	0.8	0.3	0.3
Special Purpose												
Tribal colleges	69	53	40	1	40	2	1	2	29	43	0.0	0.0
Other—special focus	83	73	4	5	2	4	7	14	0.2	0.3	3	3
Total	86	77	5	6	2	4	5	8	0.3	0.5	2	4
HBCU	31	27	57	58	1	2	9	9	0.2	0.3	1	3

AI/AN = American Indian/Alaska Native; AA/PI = Asian American/Pacific Islander.

are not that different from those found in 1993. Table 1.7 provides an additional set of abbreviated data from Table 1.5. As in 2009, two-thirds of URM faculty were at either research or baccalaureate/master's institutions in 1993. There is a three-percentage-point decline in white faculty at public research institutions, though a two-percentage-point increase at private institutions as well as in the four-year for-profit institutions. The largest change between 1993 and 2009 is for NRA faculty at private research institutions; in 1993, 21 percent of all NRA faculty were employed in these institutions. In 2009 this grew to 31 percent (declining in the public research institutions from 53 percent to 48 percent). In addition, black faculty were less likely to be employed at HBCUs in 2009 (23 percent) than in 1993 (31 percent). That shift is aligned with the decline of black faculty in public master's institutions from 23 percent to 17 percent. The distribution of black faculty was relatively stable in the other institutional types.

Discussion

Our primary goal was to study the distribution of full-time faculty by racial/ethnic and gender groups in each sector of higher education within the United States. The analysis indicated that there is a growth in the

NEW DIRECTIONS FOR INSTITUTIONAL RESEARCH • DOI: 10.1002/ir

Table 1.7. Full-Time Faculty by Institutional Type within Race/Ethnicity and Citizenship: 1993 and 2009

Institutional Type	White		Black		Latino		AA/PI		AI/AN		NRA	
	1993	2009	1993	2009	1993	2009	1993	2009	1993	2009	1993	2009
Public												
Two-year	18	18	22	22	24	24	8	8	27	24	1	3
Research	33	30	24	23	28	27	40	39	28	29	53	48
Master's	14	12	23	17	16	13	15	12	18	16	7	8
Baccalaureate	2	2	3	3	2	2	2	2	2	2	1	1
Private NFP												
Two-year	0.2	0.3	0	0	0.1	0	0	0	0	0	0	0
Research	12	14	10	12	13	14	16	20	3.8	6	21	31
MA/BA	14	14	12	13	9	9	9	7	6	7	5	5
Private For-Profit												
Two-year	0.3	1.3	0.4	3	3	3	0.2	0.6	2.3	2	0	0
Four-year	0.3	5.6	0.2	1	0.2	0.5	2.1	0.3	0.2	0.8	0	0
Special Purpose												
Tribal colleges	0.08	0.1	0	0	0	0.1	0	0	9	9	0	0
Other—special focus	6.5	6.5	5.4	6	7	7	10	12	3.5	4	11	5
Total	100	100	100	100	100	100	100	100	100	100	100	100
HBCU	0.9	0.8	31	23	1	1	5	2.4	1.3	1	1.8	1.5

AI/AN = American Indian/Alaska Native; AA/PI = Asian American/Pacific Islander.
Note: Totals may not add up to 100% due to rounding error.

number of full-time faculty overall. While this number may or may not be as large as the growth in non-full-time faculty (as in Schuster and Finkelstein, 2006), it is nonetheless worth noting. Other major findings include:

- The two-year sector has both *less* and *more* diversity—a much higher percentage of white faculty and a higher proportion of URM faculty. At the same time, this sector has a low percentage of NRA faculty.
- At the research university, the pattern reflects a lower percentage of white faculty with a much higher percentage of NRA faculty.
- There are more blacks, Latinos, and AI/AN faculty at research institutions than at two-year institutions.
- The growth of women faculty across all race/ethnic groups, international faculty, and across all sectors is significant.
- Along with an increase in white males overall (2 percent), white women account for a growing percentage of all white faculty.
- Finally, in comparing all four-year institutions versus two-year institutions, there is a much higher percentage of blacks and Latinos at four-year colleges (78 percent and 75 percent, respectively) than at all two-year institutions (22 percent and 25 percent, respectively).

As previous studies suggest (Milem and Astin, 1993; Perna, 2001, 2003), the results indicate that private four-year institutions remain among the least diverse sectors of higher education. In addition, if private for-profit or special purpose institutions such as tribal colleges and HBCUs are excluded, two-year public institutions have the largest URM representation (Milem and Astin, 1993). Also, public research institutions have the least representation of black full-time faculty. However, unlike Milem and Astin (1993), who state that blacks are best represented at public two-year institutions, our findings indicate that public baccalaureate institutions have the highest representation of blacks overall (unless we look at HBCUs separately). Furthermore, like Perna (2001), our results suggest that the gender gap is largest at research institutions. However, unlike Perna's results, which suggest that women are more likely to be employed at comprehensive institutions, our results indicate that women are relatively clustered at all levels of two-year institutions—public, private NFP, and private for-profit—while less represented at all other sectors, including public institutions. The only sector where gender is evenly distributed is at tribal colleges.

It is open to interpretation whether one views the change over time as significant, but it is clear that the racial diversity within institutional types, as well as the distribution of faculty by race across institutional types, has not changed markedly in the sixteen-year period studied. The gender distribution has changed, and, in general, women faculty grew substantially faster across all racial groups and within institutional types than men. In addition, the growth in NRA faculty is particularly noteworthy, especially at the private research universities.

NEW DIRECTIONS FOR INSTITUTIONAL RESEARCH • DOI: 10.1002/ir

Through the multilens approach, the results show how and where progress at diversifying the faculty is being made. Detailed and informative findings are presented regarding the variations among race/ethnic groups and the growth of international faculty. The slow pace of change with respect to URM faculty overall and the fast pace of change in NRA faculty might well reflect the impact of internationalization efforts in higher education. Of more concern, however, is that such movement among international faculty may also reflect an assumption that all diversities are equal and a growth in NRA can substitute for diversity among domestic faculty. This assumption is not necessarily true and can create challenges for campus diversity efforts (Smith, 2009). Moreover, the fact that many campuses do not disaggregate NRA faculty can suggest more diversity of domestic blacks, Latinos, and Asian Americans than might be the case.

By using multiple lenses on population-based data and by disaggregating our findings by race/ethnicity, gender, citizenship, and institutional types, our research portrays the American faculty in significantly more detail than previous studies. Our findings debunk the myths that faculty of color are largely clustered at two-year institutions (Alex-Assensoh, 2003; Allen and others, 2002; Contreras, 1998; Slaughter, 2007). The results demonstrate some profound changes with respect to gender and international faculty and some progress, albeit too slow for the contemporary society, in the presence of historically underrepresented faculty. Moreover, the findings illustrate the importance of looking at faculty diversity by institutional type and underscore for institutional research the importance of disaggregating data not only by race/ethnicity and gender but by citizenship status as well.

Institutional researchers are often called upon to examine and report to internal and external audiences how patterns in faculty hiring and diversification have changed over time at their respective institutions. Findings from this study also suggest that in doing so, institutional researchers ought to account for the larger pattern of changes taking place throughout the country and, most important, within their college's specific institutional type. Institutional researchers may utilize our findings as initial "benchmarks of faculty diversification" by which to compare their institution's efforts in diversifying their full-time faculty. By doing so, researchers may influence institutional policy pertaining to the faculty hiring process, which may lead to intentionally seeking out a more diverse pool of candidates.

Notes

1. We have opted to use the term Latino(s) to refer to individuals who are reported in the literature and in government data sets (for example, IPEDS) as Hispanic(s), Latino(s), or in some instances, to an individual ethnicity. However, we fully recognize that Hispanic/Latino Americans are very racially diverse.

NEW DIRECTIONS FOR INSTITUTIONAL RESEARCH • DOI: 10.1002/ir

2. Please contact the authors for more details about the categorization of the institutions.

References

Allen, W. R., and others. "Outsiders Within: Race, Gender, and Faculty Status in U.S. Higher Education." In W. A. Smith, P. G. Altbach, and K. Lomotey (eds.), *The Racial Crisis in American Higher Education: Continuing Challenges for the Twenty-First Century* (rev. ed.). Albany: State University of New York Press, 2002.

Alex-Assensoh, Y. "Race in the Academy: Moving Beyond Diversity and Toward the Incorporation of Faculty of Color in Predominantly White Colleges and Universities." *Journal of Black Studies*, 2003, *34*(1), 5–11.

Antonio, A. L. "Faculty of Color Reconsidered." *Journal of Higher Education*, 2002, *73*(5), 582–602.

Bower, B. L. "Campus Life for Faculty of Color: Still Strangers After All These Years?" *New Directions for Community Colleges*, 2002, *118*, 79–88.

Contreras, A. R. "Leading From the Margins in the Ivory Tower." In L. A. Valverde and L. A. Castenell (eds.), *The Multicultural Campus: Strategies for Transforming Higher Education*. Walnut Creek, Calif.: AltaMira Press, 1998.

Gahn, S., and Twombly, S. B. "Dimensions of the Community College Labor Market." *Review of Higher Education*, 2001, *24*, 259–282.

Mamiseishvili, K., and Rosser, V. J. "Examining the Relationship Between Faculty Productivity and Job Satisfaction." *Journal of the Professoriate*, 2011, *5*(2), 100–132.

Milem, J., and Astin, H. "The Changing Composition of the Faculty: What Does It Really Mean for Diversity?" *Change*, 1993, *25*(2), 21–27.

Perna, L. W. "Sex Differences in Faculty Salaries: A Cohort Analysis." *Review of Higher Education*, 2001, *24*, 283–307.

Perna, L. W. "The Status of Women and Minorities Among Community College Faculty." *Research in Higher Education*, 2003, *44*(2), 205–240.

Perna, L. W., Gerald, D., Baum, E., and Milem, J. "The Status of Equity for Black Faculty and Administrators in Public Higher Education in the South." *Journal of the Association for Institutional Research*, 2007, *48*(2), 193–228.

Schuster, J. H., and Finkelstein, M. J. *The American Faculty: Restructuring Academic Work and Careers*. Baltimore, Md.: Johns Hopkins University Press, 2006.

Seidman, E. *In the Words of the Faculty: Perspectives on Improving Teaching and Educational Quality in Community College*. San Francisco: Jossey-Bass, 1985.

Slaughter, J. B. "Creating a Faculty of Equity and Excellence: Recruiting, Retaining, and Advancing Faculty of Color." Presentation at the Keeping Our Faculties IV National Symposium, Minneapolis, Minn., April 2007.

Smith, D. G. *Diversity's Promise for Higher Education: Making It Work*. Baltimore, Md.: Johns Hopkins University Press, 2009.

Smith, W. A., Altbach, P. G., and Lomotey, K. *The Racial Crisis in American Higher Education: Continuing Challenges for the Twenty-First Century*. New York: State University of New York Press, 2002.

Snyder, T. D., Dillow, S. A., and Hoffman, C. M. *Digest of Education Statistics 2008* (NCES 2009-020). Washington, D.C.: National Center for Education Statistics, Institute of Education Sciences, U.S. Department of Education, 2009.

Townsend, B. K. "Women Community College Faculty: On the Margins or in the Mainstream?" *New Directions for Community Colleges*, 1995, *89*, 39–46.

Townsend, B. K. "Women Faculty: Satisfaction with Employment in the Community College." *Community College Journal of Research and Practice*, 1998, *22*(7), 655–661.

Trower, C. A., and Chait, R. "Faculty Diversity: Too Little for Too Long." *Harvard Magazine*, 2002, *104*(4), 33–37.

Turner, C.S.V., Gonzalez, J. C., and Wood, J. L. "Faculty of Color in Academe: What 20 Years of Literature Tells Us." *Journal of Diversity in Higher Education,* 2008, *1*(3), 139–168.

Twombly, S. B. "What We Know About Women at Community Colleges: An Examination of the Literature Using Feminist Phase Theory." *Journal of Higher Education,* 1993, *64*, 186–211.

Wolf-Wendel, L., Ward, K., and Twombly, S. B. "Faculty Life at Community Colleges: The Perspective of Women With Children." *Community College Review,* 2007, *34*(4), 255–281.

DARYL G. SMITH *is a professor of education and psychology at Claremont Graduate University. Daryl can be reached at daryl.smith@cgu.edu.*

ESAU TOVAR *is a doctoral student at Claremont Graduate University and associate professor of counseling at Santa Monica College.*

HUGO A. GARCÍA *is a doctoral student at Claremont Graduate University.*

NEW DIRECTIONS FOR INSTITUTIONAL RESEARCH • DOI: 10.1002/ir

2

The increasing presence of international faculty members is validated using multiple data sources, and their professional experience is examined in terms of the perception of academic life, productivity, and career mobility.

International Faculty in American Universities: Experiences of Academic Life, Productivity, and Career Mobility

Dongbin Kim, Susan Twombly, and Lisa Wolf-Wendel

In the past twenty years, the number of international faculty members at American universities has continued to increase rapidly. This increase is due in large part to changes in U.S. immigration laws in the 1990s that allowed for "highly skilled" workers, especially those with doctorates, to immigrate to the United States (Johnson, 2000; Lowell, 2001; Watts, 2001). The number of full-time foreign-born faculty members in 1969 was 28,200 (10 percent of total), increasing to 74,200 (15.5 percent) in 1998 and reaching 126,123 in 2007 (Marvasti, 2005; "Open Doors 2008," 2008; Schuster and Finkelstein, 2006). Foreign-born faculty are concentrated in the natural science and engineering fields, accounting for 20.9 percent of faculty in these fields (35 percent of faculty in engineering and 39 percent in computer science). In 2003, 51 percent of doctoral recipients in science and engineering fields in the United States were foreign-born (Bound, Turner, and Walsh, 2009). With the strikingly large percentages of doctoral degrees awarded to foreign-born individuals, the proportional representation of foreign-born faculty—particularly in science, technology, engineering, and math (STEM) fields—will only continue to grow (Hoffer, Hess, Welch, and Williams, 2006).

This growth is evident in data showing that the proportional representation of foreign-born faculty easily surpasses that of domestic underrepresented racial/ethnic groups. Drawing from the most recent data from

NEW DIRECTIONS FOR INSTITUTIONAL RESEARCH, no. 155, Fall 2012 © Wiley Periodicals, Inc.
Published online in Wiley Online Library (wileyonlinelibrary.com) • DOI: 10.1002/ir.20020

the National Center for Education Statistics (NCES), for example, of the 11,599 new tenure-track (assistant professor level) faculty at four-year degree-granting institutions in 2009, 11.5 percent (1,332) were nonresident aliens, higher than Asian American (10.5 percent), African American (0.5 percent), and Hispanic (0.4 percent) representations (author's own calculation with Integrated Postsecondary Education Data System [IPEDS], 2009).

Despite their increasing presence, scholarly attention to international faculty has been limited and is just now gaining attention. Little is known about who they are and how they experience U.S. higher education institutions. This chapter aims to begin to fill the gap in our knowledge by offering a descriptive overview of this little-known segment of American professoriate. We present descriptive statistics drawn from multiple data sources including the Survey of Doctorate Recipients (SDR: 2003) collected by the National Science Foundation, Pretenure Faculty COACHE (2005–2008) data by Harvard Graduate School of Education, IPEDS (2009 and 2010) and the National Survey of Postsecondary Faculty (NSOPF: 1993, 1999, and 2004), both maintained by NCES.

These different data sets have distinct strengths and weaknesses in explaining international faculty, so to generate comparable findings, we have focused on individuals who work at four-year colleges and universities in the United States who hold tenure-track faculty positions in biological/medical science, physical science, computer science, engineering, and social sciences. This is not to say that the representation of international faculty in humanities and professional fields is also not growing. In fact, as Table 2.1 indicates, the percentage distributions of international faculty range from 8.9 percent in education to 42.6 percent in engineering. Nearly 20 percent of faculty in humanities and medical/health professions and 31 percent of business faculty are noncitizen faculty. However, because of the focus of some of the available data sets, namely, SDR, and because of the attention given to faculty in STEM fields, this chapter will primarily focus on international faculty in the physical/biological sciences, engineering, technology, mathematics, and social sciences (including economics and education). Those in humanities and professional fields (including medical/health professions and business) are not included in further analysis unless otherwise specified.

Definitions of International Faculty

The primary interest of this chapter on international faculty and their professional experiences in U.S. higher education institutions is based on the assumption that international faculty are considered to be different than domestic faculty in their academic experiences, largely due to their cultural, educational, and language backgrounds. However, the first challenge is to define what we mean by international faculty. Most research on international

NEW DIRECTIONS FOR INSTITUTIONAL RESEARCH • DOI: 10.1002/ir

Table 2.1. Percentage Distributions of International Faculty by Academic Disciplines (COACHE 2005–2008, n = 14,543)

	% of Total (n)	U.S. Citizen	Noncitizen
Humanities	14.2% (2,065)	80.9	19.1
Social sciences	17.4% (2,525)	83.9	16.1
Physical sciences	6.5% (943)	66.8	33.2
Biological sciences	5.2% (750)	76.8	23.2
Visual and performing arts	6.7% (972)	88.2	11.8
Engineering/computer sciences	12.0% (1,750)	57.4	42.6
Health and human ecology	4.2% (613)	82.9	17.1
Agriculture/environment sciences	4.4% (641)	77.1	22.9
Business	6.4% (934)	68.5	31.5
Education	7.5% (1,097)	91.1	8.9
Medical/health professions	8.5% (1,237)	81.2	18.8
Other professions	7.0% (1,016)	85.2	14.8

faculty defines them by place of birth (foreign-born) or by citizenship (non-U.S. citizens). These definitions may over- or underestimate the representation of international faculty and thus generate misleading results on the effects of this status on various work life variables. For example, studies using citizenship (that is, non-U.S. citizens) as the definition (see, for example, Mamiseishvili and Rosser, 2011) exclude many faculty members who were born and educated abroad but who have become naturalized U.S. citizens, thus underreporting the number of international faculty.

Among the foreign-born faculty in the 2003 SDR, two-thirds (64.1 percent) are actually U.S. citizens; about 40 percent completed their undergraduate education in the United States, while 60 percent were educated in a foreign country. Studies using birthplace do not take into account when the individual immigrated to the United States. Anyone born outside of the United States is considered "international" regardless of citizenship or how long they have lived in the United States and where they were educated. However, a sizeable percentage of foreign-born faculty members came to the United States as teenagers, earning their bachelor's degree at a U.S. university. These individuals may be very different culturally and linguistically than foreign-born faculty who remained in their home country for their undergraduate degree. These definitional problems may blur important differences between U.S. and international faculty members. In addition to birthplace or citizenship status, some databases (including IPEDS from the Department of Education) use nonresident alien (NRA) status as a way to define internationals. While an alien is any person who is not a citizen of the United States, a clear distinction is made by the federal government between a resident and an NRA. On one hand, a resident alien legally means someone with permanent residency. A nonresident alien, on the other hand, is someone with temporary visa status.

NEW DIRECTIONS FOR INSTITUTIONAL RESEARCH • DOI: 10.1002/ir

For example, students or scholars with F-1 or J-1 visa status will be considered NRAs until they have established permanent residence status.

According to Kerr and Lincoln (2008), the H-1B visa (NRA status) and permanent residency (resident alien status) are the most common statuses for foreign-born faculty. According to the IPEDS definition, faculty with permanent residency are considered resident aliens and therefore not counted as international. Many higher education institutions grant a tenured appointment only for the individual who has obtained permanent resident status. In addition, large numbers of foreign-born faculty, particularly among those at the senior rank, are naturalized U.S. citizens. Therefore, categorizing international faculty members as only those who are NRAs may result in a significant underestimate of the representation of foreign-born or non-U.S. citizen international faculty. Because the various data sets offer different ways of identifying international faculty status, this chapter uses multiple definitions of international faculty depending on the data used.

In our own research on international faculty using the SDR (Kim, Wolf-Wendel, and Twombly, 2011), we divided foreign-born faculty according to whether they earned their undergraduate degrees in their home country or in the United States. In so doing, we assume that foreign-born faculty who earned undergraduate degrees in their country of birth may have very different cultural, social, and educational experiences that affect their academic life than their foreign born counterparts who received their undergraduate education in the United States. This distinction is particularly relevant given that the majority of college populations are undergraduates, and faculty's primary work responsibility is teaching or working with undergraduates: having college experiences as a student in U.S. higher education institutions could significantly affect faculty members' overall experience in academia.

While the COACHE and NSOPF data sets provide extensive information about faculty experiences and perceptions of their work environment, they offer only a citizenship variable as an indicator of international status. The limitation of defining international faculty by their citizenship status is somewhat minimized when COACHE data are used, given that it includes only pretenure faculty, and the majority of pretenure foreign born faculty are non-U.S. citizens compared to 80 percent of tenured foreign-born faculty who are naturalized citizens.

As the different data sets that we use in this chapter allow for various definitions to be employed, we will note the definition used as we present the various data.

International Faculty

Who They Are. According to the SDR (2003), of the selected tenure-track faculty at four-year institutions, slightly less than 80 percent (n = 5,527) are U.S.-born with U.S. undergraduate degrees. Of the foreign born faculty, 31 percent (n = 424) are foreign-born with U.S. undergraduate degrees and 69 percent (n = 987) are foreign-born with foreign undergraduate degrees. Similar patterns are found by citizenship status. Of the faculty respondents to the pretenure faculty COACHE survey from 2005 to 2008, 23 percent (n = 1,681) were non-U.S. citizen faculty.

Of the foreign-born foreign educated (FBFD) faculty, the largest numbers are from countries in Asia (62.3 percent), followed by Europe (17.2 percent), Africa (6.3 percent), and North America (5.2 percent). On the other hand, among foreign-born U.S. educated (FBUSD), 42 percent are from Asian countries, 31.6 percent are from Europe, Africa (7.3 percent), and the Caribbean (6.1 percent). More specifically, while nearly half the FBFD faculty members are from Asian countries, including China (20.3 percent), India (20.2 percent), and Taiwan (5.4 percent), the countries of origin are more geographically diverse among FBUSD. The largest percentages are from Germany (9.4 percent), followed by Iran (5.2 percent), Canada (5.2 percent), and Greece (4.5 percent). Only 4 percent and 3.5 percent, respectively, of the FBUSD are from China and India. In sum, FBUSD and FBFD present quite different demographic profiles; FBUSD are in many ways more like U.S.-born and -educated faculty members. These findings support our argument that definitions of international faculty matter. It is likely inaccurate to lump FBFD and FBUSD together. Our research suggests they need to be considered separately, not only because of their educational backgrounds but, more important, because of the differences in the cultural, social, and language backgrounds related to their countries of origin and the location in which they received their undergraduate degree.

Table 2.2 presents the individual and educational characteristics of FBUSD and FBFD compared with U.S. faculty. While 27 percent of U.S. faculty and 26 percent of FBUSD faculty are female, only 17 percent of FBFD faculty are female. FBFD faculty are most likely to have spouses who are not working at all (28.4 percent) as compared to FBUSD faculty (19.8 percent) and U.S. faculty (22.9 percent), and the differences are statistically significant at the .001 level. On the other hand, FBFD faculty members are least likely to be single/not married (14.5 percent) compared with FBUSD (21.8 percent) or U.S. faculty (18.2 percent). Institutional selectivity of the doctoral degree-granting institutions does not present statistically significant differences across faculty's international status. The highest percentage of FBUSD faculty (70.2 percent) received their doctoral degrees from highly selective institutions, compared with 65 percent of U.S. faculty and 66 percent of FBFD faculty.

Where They Work. As to the field of study, significantly higher percentages of faculty in physical sciences (33.2 percent), engineering and computer sciences (42.6 percent), and business (31.5 percent) are internationals (noncitizens). In contrast, less than 9 percent of faculty members

NEW DIRECTIONS FOR INSTITUTIONAL RESEARCH • DOI: 10.1002/ir

Table 2.2. Percentage Distributions of International Faculty by Individual Characteristics (SDR: 2003)

| | Descriptive Statistics | | | |
Variables	FBFD faculty	FBUSD faculty	U.S. Faculty	p Value
Who They Are				
Gender (female)	17.1%	25.7%	26.5%	***
Marriage and spouse working status				***
Married with working full-time spouse	43.1%	44.3%	43.1%	
Married with working part-time spouse	14.0%	14.2%	15.8%	
Married with not working spouse	28.4%	19.8%	22.9%	
Not married	14.5%	21.8%	18.2%	
Institutional selectivity (doctoral institution)				ns
Least selective	2.9%	2.4%	2.3%	
Selective	30.8%	27.4%	32.2%	
Highly selective	66.3%	70.2%	65.4%	
Where They Work				
Institutional selectivity (current institution)				ns
Least selective	23.5%	27.0%	25.9%	
Selective	33.8%	28.4%	30.5%	
Highly selective	42.8%	44.6%	43.7%	
Size of the city (current institution)				***
Large city	40.2%	41.2%	32.5%	
Mid-size city	36.7%	31.5%	41.0%	
Small city	12.0%	14.9%	11.8%	
Other area (including rural)	11.1%	12.5%	14.7%	

% of international faculty	0.026	0.024	0.023	***
% of international students	0.072	0.070	0.060	***
	(−2.94)	(−2.99)	(−3.12)	
Number of doctoral degrees awarded	258.65	248.85	248.22	ns
Major Field				***
Engineering	27.2%	22.6%	15.1%	
Computer and math field	18.7%	10.4%	8.2%	
Bio, agricultural, and environment	15.9%	18.9%	25.0%	
Physical and related fields	24.9%	31.4%	36.9%	
Social and related fields	13.0%	16.7%	14.7%	
What They Experience				
Satisfaction with workplace conditions	14.14	14.37	14.48	***
Satisfaction with salary and benefits	6.04	6.06	6.19	**
Productivity[a]	0.96 (−0.49)	0.70 (−0.79)	0.60 (−0.95)	***

$*p < 0.05, **p < 0.01, ***p < 0.000$

[a]For categorical variables, a series of chi-square tests of distribution was conducted. For continuous variables, a series of ANOVA was conducted. Numbers in parentheses for the productivity and percentage of international students at the institutions are log-transformed due to the violations of homogeneity of variances assumption.

Sources: Data are weighted using relative weight (Thomas and Heck, 2001). Institute for Scientific Information, Inc. and National Science Foundation, Division of Science Resource Statistics, Special tabulations. The use of NSF data does not imply NSF endorsement of the research methods or conclusions contained in this report.

Table 2.3. Percentages of Nonresident Alien Faculty: Selected Twenty Institutions (IPEDS Faculty data: 2010)

	% Not Tenured	% Tenured
Pennsylvania State University–Penn State Mont Alto	50	0
Kent State University at Trumbull	40	7
University of Texas at Austin	35	15
Clarkson University	31	1
Missouri University of Science and Technology	31	3
University of South Carolina–Columbia	29	11
Princeton University	29	0
Colorado State University–Fort Collins	28	7
Georgetown University	28	12
University of Massachusetts–Dartmouth	27	1
Oklahoma State University—main campus	26	6
SUNY Maritime College	26	0
Teachers College at Columbia University	25	5
Colorado School of Mines	24	0
Denison University	24	4
Wright State University—main campus	24	8
University of Texas Medical Branch	24	2
Texas A & M University–Texarkana	23	3
Purdue University–Calumet campus	23	0
Louisiana Tech University	23	8
University at Buffalo	23	0
Stony Brook University	22	1
University of North Dakota	22	8
Colgate University	21	10
University of St. Thomas	21	7

in the field of education are internationals (see Table 2.1). Significantly different patterns of distribution across fields of study are also found among foreign-born versus U.S. faculty. While larger percentages of FBFD faculty are employed in the field of computer/math or engineering than U.S. faculty, U.S. faculty members are more likely to be employed in biology or physical science than are foreign-born faculty. Slightly higher percentages of FBUSD faculty are employed in the social sciences than FBFD or U.S. faculty (see Table 2.2).

Table 2.3 presents data from the top twenty-five four-year public or private, not-for-profit institutions that have the highest percentages of international faculty among their regular, full-time, and tenure-track (but not tenured) faculty from IPEDS faculty and staff data in 2010. It is very obvious that there are significant differences in the distributions of international faculty by their tenure status. For example, while 15 percent of all tenured faculty members at University of Texas at Austin are internationals (that is, NRAs with temporary visa status), 35 percent of the faculty who are on tenure probation are classified as international. These patterns are consistent across all institutions, indicating that international faculty

NEW DIRECTIONS FOR INSTITUTIONAL RESEARCH • DOI: 10.1002/ir

are more represented among newly hired on tenure-track assistant rank than in tenured positions. This pattern might be related to the definition of internationals in IPEDS data: only the individuals with temporary visa status are considered internationals. It is worth noting that, of these top twenty-five institutions, there are significant variations in terms of the type or size of the institutions, ranging from large public institutions (for example, UT Austin or Colorado State University) to highly selective private research institutions (for example, Georgetown or Princeton University) to small public institutions (for example, Kent State University or Pennsylvania State University–Penn State New Kensington).

The prevalence of international faculty is not limited to a certain sector of U.S. higher education institutions but is widespread among a range of institution types. The descriptive statistics from SDR data also show that there is no significantly different pattern in the selectivity of the institutions where faculty members work by their international faculty status. However, foreign-born faculty members (regardless of where they received their undergraduate degree) are more likely than U.S. faculty to work at institutions that are located in larger cities, at institutions that award more doctoral degrees, and at more internationalized campuses (in terms of the percentage of international faculty and international students; Kim, Wolf-Wendel, and Twombly, 2011).

What They Experience in Terms of Satisfaction and Productivity. Given that the prevalence of international faculty is significantly different by field of study, faculty's professional experiences may also be significantly different by field of study even among the foreign-born faculty. Satisfaction or morale is an important variable to study for faculty because it has been found to affect performance (Levine and Strauss, 1989; Mamisheishvili and Rosser, 2011) as well as turnover (Johnsrud and Rosser, 2002; Rosser, 2004; Smart, 1990; Zhou and Volkwein, 2004). Interestingly, research on international faculty morale reveals a paradox. International faculty are less satisfied than their U.S.-born colleagues while being more productive (Corley and Sabharwal, 2007; Kim and others, 2011; Levin and Stephan, 1999; Mamiseishvili and Rosser, 2011; Wells and others, 2007). Our analysis of SDR data confirmed earlier findings that U.S. faculty members are more satisfied than foreign-born faculty but less productive in terms of publication rates (see Table 2.2). More specifically, FBFD faculty are significantly less satisfied than U.S. faculty but more productive as measured by annualized publication rates. Interestingly, the same differences are not found in comparisons between FBUSD and U.S. faculty. This holds true even after controlling for relevant individual demographic and professional experience variables in a multivariate analysis (Kim, Wolf-Wendel, and Twombly, 2011). All things being equal, FBFD faculty members are significantly more productive than U.S. faculty, and the difference is significant at the 0.01 level. FBUSD faculty, however, are not different from U.S. faculty in their productivity.

Productivity notwithstanding, several recent qualitative studies of the experiences of international faculty conclude that pretenure international faculty feel the same kinds of stress as U.S. faculty. International faculty experienced additional concerns, including problems dealing with immigration rules and regulations; different cultural values; discrimination; difficulty in socialization and interaction with colleagues, administrators, and students; and the challenge of determining both implicit and explicit academic expectations (Skachkova, 2007; Theobald, 2007; Thomas and Johnson, 2004). In addition, Manrique and Manrique (1999) concluded that international faculty often experience being a "minority" or a "person of color" for the first time when they are in the United States. Add to this that many students perceive international faculty as "foreign" and "less credible, less intelligible" and even less intelligent due to their status as non-native speakers of English (Manrique and Manrique, 1999; McCalman, 2007).

To have a deeper understanding of why there are significant differences in faculty satisfaction and productivity by international status, we explored COACHE data of pretenure faculty for a series of faculty perception of and satisfaction with institutional policy and programs (see Table 2.4). Noncitizen faculty considered tenure processes at their universities (including the body of evidence required for the tenure decision and the likelihood of achieving tenure) to be clearer than U.S. faculty did ($p <$ 0.05). We also found that noncitizen faculty are more satisfied with research-related measures (including the amount of time that faculty have to conduct research and the expectation of securing external funding) than U.S. faculty ($p < 0.001$). It is particularly worth noting that faculty satisfaction with the composite measure of teaching is almost identical for U.S. and non-U.S. faculty (4.01 and 4.00, respectively). While U.S. faculty are more satisfied with the interactions with their departmental and institutional colleagues and more satisfied with their department and

Table 2.4. Mean Comparisons Between U.S. Citizen and Non-U.S. Citizen Faculty (COACHE, N = 5,748)

	U.S. Citizen	Non-U.S. Citizen	t Value
Perception of tenure	3.68	3.75	−2.310*
Satisfaction with teaching	4.01	4.00	0.237, ns
Satisfaction with research expectation	2.76	3.22	−10.655***
Satisfaction with research funding expectation	3.09	3.17	−2.129*
Satisfaction with salary	3.25	3.26	−0.391, ns
Satisfaction with fit	3.83	3.71	3.460**
Overall satisfaction	3.89	3.86	1.143, ns

Note: Variables are on five-point scales from 1 to 5.
$*t < 0.05$; $**t < 0.01$; $***t < 0.001$

New Directions for Institutional Research • DOI: 10.1002/ir

Table 2.5. Means of Professional Experiences by the Field of Study, Among Non-U.S. Citizen Faculty (COACHE)

	Social Sciences	Physical Sciences	Biological Sciences	Engineering	Education
Perception of tenure	3.63	3.80	3.66	3.74	3.63
Satisfaction with teaching	3.88	4.00	3.78	3.91	3.82
Satisfaction with research expectation	2.98	3.19	2.94	3.32	2.92
Satisfaction with research funding expectation	3.11	3.25	3.03	3.08	2.96
Satisfaction with salary	3.58	3.75	3.66	3.57	3.48
Satisfaction with fit	3.16	3.21	3.14	3.29	2.70
Overall satisfaction	3.79	3.81	3.68	3.73	3.68

Note: Variables are on five-point scales from 1 to 5.

institution as a workplace than noncitizen faculty, only satisfaction with the interaction with other colleagues presented significant differences by citizenship status, indicating that noncitizen faculty are less satisfied with collegial interaction than U.S. faculty ($p < 0.01$).

International faculty members are not evenly distributed across different fields of study but heavily focused on physical sciences and engineering. It is apparent that noncitizen faculty in physical sciences and engineering are consistently more satisfied with all measures of professional experiences than their counterpart international faculty in education or social sciences (see Table 2.5). International faculty in education are particularly less satisfied with their departmental or institutional fit (that is, interaction with department or institutional colleagues) than international faculty in any other field. This might be due to their relatively low numbers in the discipline. However, all international faculty, regardless of the field of study, show very similar levels of overall satisfaction.

Changes in Profile and Experiences of International Faculty over Time

The NSOPF data provide a unique benefit for comparing international faculty over the years since the data were collected repeatedly in 1992–1993, 1998–1999, and 2003–2004. NSOPF data define international faculty as being non-U.S. citizens and therefore include both the FBFD and FBUSD in the same category. The top five countries that sent the largest numbers of international faculty remain exactly same for the 1993 and 1999 faculty cohorts (United Kingdom, India, Canada, Germany, and China). However, the percentage representations by countries changed rather significantly over this time period. Among the 1999 cohort, China ranked first (13.7

Table 2.6. Changes in the Characteristics of International Faculty (NSOPF: 1993, 1999, and 2004)

		1993	1999	2004
Authority deciding course content	United States	3.71	3.74**	
	International	3.65	3.66	
Authority making other job decisions	United States	3.09	3.05*	3.77
	International	3.10	2.96	3.65*
Authority deciding courses taught	United States	3.30**	3.37***	
	International	3.19	3.22	
Time available to advise students	United States	3.09	3.05	
	International	3.14	3.02	
Quality of undergraduates	United States	2.90***	2.84***	
	International	2.73	2.56	
Quality of graduate students	United States	3.06**	3.06***	
	International	2.93	2.85	
Workload	United States	2.91	2.80*	2.94
	International	3.00	2.71	2.94
Job security	United States	3.34***	3.49***	
	International	3.15	3.28	
Advancement opportunity	United States	3.05	3.13	
	International	3.07	3.04*	
Time keeping current in field	United States	2.58*	2.51	
	International	2.69	2.49	
Free to do outside consulting	United States	3.16*	3.20**	
	International	3.07	3.10	
Salary	United States	2.50	2.57***	2.64
	International	2.49	2.41	2.61
Benefits	United States	2.91	3.02*	3.02*
	International	2.85	2.93	2.95
Spouse employment opportunity	United States	2.93***	3.01***	
	International	2.57	2.69	
Overall job satisfaction	United States	3.14	3.16**	3.24**
	International	3.13	3.06	3.15

Note: All variables indicate "satisfaction with ..." on five-point scales from 1 to 5 (least satisfied to very satisfied).
$*p < 0.05; **p < 0.01; ***p < 0.001$

percent), a jump from fifth among the 1993 cohort (5.4 percent). The percentage representations of international faculty from the United Kingdom, India, and Germany declined slightly from 1993 to 1999. In all three time periods, the ratio of tenured versus nontenured faculty has remained relatively stable: about 40 percent to 50 percent of international faculty are tenured compared with more than 70 percent of U.S. faculty.

Based on NSOPF data, Table 2.6 presents a series of faculty satisfaction variables by the citizenship status over time. In general, U.S. faculty are more satisfied than international faculty members with many aspects of faculty satisfaction measures. This pattern is consistent throughout the three administrations of the NSOPF survey. International faculty are less satisfied than U.S. faculty with the quality of students (both undergraduate and graduate students). This difference might be related to an artifact of the interaction (negative interaction, in particular) between international faculty and students or due to the lack of familiarity with the characteristics or the quality of the students with whom they teach and interact. U.S. faculty are also significantly more satisfied with job security than international faculty. This is, in part, related to the difference in tenure status: higher percentages of U.S. faculty are tenured and thus they may feel more secure than their counterpart international faculty. International faculty are less satisfied with spousal employment opportunities than U.S. faculty, and this tendency is consistent over the two time points (1993 and 1999). Finally, international faculty are consistently less satisfied with their job overall than U.S. faculty, and this is true over the three time points. While the difference by the citizenship status is not statistically significant in 1993, the gaps become greater and are statistically significant in 1999 and 2004.

Faculty Mobility: Intent to Leave Versus Actual Departure

Faculty mobility has long been a topic of interest to both higher education policymakers and researchers, due in part to the significant financial and educational consequences it has for institutions. High faculty turnover rates can be directly translated into lost income due to the investment the institutions have made in their faculty. This is particularly true in STEM fields for which universities invest significant amounts of start-up funds, ranging from an average of $390,000 to $490,000 at the assistant professor level and about $700,000 to $1.44 million at the senior faculty level (Ehrenberg, Rizzo, and Condie, 2003). As a result of turnover, institutions also confront discontinuity in their research and educational programs, the additional cost of recruiting and mentoring new faculty members, and the investment of additional start-up funds for replacement faculty (Ehrenberg, Kasper, and Rees, 1991; Xu, 2008).

In much of the prior research, faculty mobility is measured by intention to leave due to the lack of appropriate variables (for example, actual mobility) in nationally representative sample data (for example, NSOPF or COACHE). Using the COACHE pretenure faculty data, we examined faculty intent to leave and its relationship with faculty satisfaction with and perceptions of departmental/institutional fit (see Table 2.7). Significant differences by international status emerged. About 83.1 percent of U.S. citizen faculty plan to remain at the same institution assuming they achieve tenure, in comparison to 78.8 percent of noncitizen faculty with the same plan (chi-square = 10.813, $p < 0.001$). Also, 68 percent of U.S. faculty who plan to leave their institution within five years after they get tenure do so because they prefer to work at another academic institution, as

Table 2.7. Mean Comparisons in Faculty Satisfaction with Their Colleagues: By Citizenship Status (COACHE, n = 5,748)

	Faculty Who Intend to Leave	Faculty Who Intend to Stay	t Value
Satisfaction with tenured faculty in the department/institution	3.74	2.90	20.125***
Satisfaction with pre-tenured faculty in the department/institution	4.01	3.48	14.454***
Belongingness or comfort with department/institution	4.11	3.00	28.681***

	Faculty Who Intend to Stay		
	U.S. Citizen	Non-U.S. Citizen	t Value
Satisfaction with tenured faculty in the department/institution	3.75	3.74	0.252, ns
Satisfaction with pretenured faculty in the department/institution	4.03	3.91	3.179**
Belongingness or comfort with department/institution	4.11	4.13	−0.400, ns

	Faculty Who Intend to Leave		
	U.S. Citizen	Non-U.S. Citizen	t Value
Satisfaction with tenured faculty in the department/institution	2.96	2.81	1.390, ns
Satisfaction with pretenured faculty in the department/institution	3.59	3.20	4.11***
Belongingness or comfort with department/institution	3.04	2.95	0.850, ns

Note: Variables are on five-point scales from 1 to 5.
*$t < 0.05$; **$t < 0.01$; ***$t < 0.001$

compared to a significantly higher 80 percent of non-U.S. citizen faculty. Because noncitizen faculty are significantly less satisfied with their interaction with other colleagues (particularly with pretenured faculty), this finding suggests that international faculty may experience difficulties in relating with other colleagues in their department and institution. This speculation is supported by the statistics that show different patterns in faculty satisfaction measures by their intent to leave. Faculty who have intentions to leave are significantly less satisfied with all three measures of faculty satisfaction with their interaction or comfort level in the department or institutions than their counterparts who have no intentions to leave.

NEW DIRECTIONS FOR INSTITUTIONAL RESEARCH • DOI: 10.1002/ir

Using the COACHE data, we also found statistically significant differences by citizenship status in faculty's response to whether they had thought about either staying or leaving yet. While less than 20 percent of U.S. faculty indicated that they had not thought about leaving, nearly twice the percentage (37 percent) of noncitizen faculty said the same. This may indicate that noncitizen faculty were much more likely not to be clear about their future (in terms of moving or staying) or they tended to have a wait-and-see attitude until things get clearer (for example, successfully achieving tenure). A further descriptive analysis shows that, regardless of citizenship status, faculty who have not thought about their departure yet were consistently in the middle range of all variables regarding faculty perceptions of and satisfaction with professional experiences. In other words, faculty without clear departure intentions (or stay intentions) tend to have higher satisfaction with teaching-related measures, research commitment, expectations for external funding, institutional fit, salary level, workplace, and tenure procedure than those who had clear intentions to leave. This indecisive group also had lower satisfaction levels than those who had clear intentions to stay. These differences across three responses (not determined, clear intentions to stay, and clear intentions to leave) were statistically significant at the .001 level.

The faculty labor market is highly segmented, and mobility is restricted by institutional type and academic field. Nonetheless, faculty do have the option either to leave for another higher education institution (that is, stay within academia) or to move to industry, thereby leaving academia entirely. International faculty have these options at their disposal as well as one that their U.S.-born counterparts do not have: the ability to go home. As other countries rush to invest in creating world-class research universities (for example, the "211" and "985" projects in China are the two major government-initiated efforts that are specifically intended to recruit scholars overseas in its movements to build world-class universities), returning home may become a more attractive option for international faculty.

The longitudinal component of the SDR offers data on actual departure patterns that include both the mobility within academia and mobility to the nonacademic sector. Unfortunately, the SDR has not tracked international faculty members who have left the United States. Of the total sample (n = 6,799), 83 percent stayed in the same institution between 2001 and 2003. Of those who left their institutions during this time period, 55 percent (n = 621) moved to another higher education institution and 45 percent (n = 517) moved out of academia and went to industry. While foreign-born and U.S.-born faculty present similar stay rates (82 percent and 84 percent, respectively), among those who left their institutions, different mobility patterns by foreign-born faculty status emerged. Of the 233 foreign-born faculty members who left their institution, 55 percent (n = 128) left academia and went to industry, while about 43 percent (n = 905) of U.S.-born faculty who left did the same. In other words, while foreign-born faculty are not necessarily different from U.S.-born faculty in terms of their mobility within academia, they are significantly more likely to go to industry, leaving academia entirely. Little previous research has examined this multiple postdeparture pattern in terms of actual mobility. Therefore, the unique pattern of actual mobility, particularly for international faculty, certainly expands our current knowledge of faculty mobility, which tends to be focused on a more dichotomous measure of departure versus staying put.

Implications for Institutional Policymakers and Researchers

This descriptive portrait of international faculty in the United States is important as a base for future research but also for institutions with larger numbers of international faculty wishing to tailor policy, procedures, and professional development opportunities to this unique group of faculty. Not only will international faculty members contribute to U.S. scientific productivity but, in their teaching role, they will be key in preparing future generations of the U.S. population and labor force. Indeed, international faculty members are educating a large percentage of U.S. college students, thus influencing the United States' future economic capacity. They are also making significant contributions to scientific knowledge. The presence of international faculty in the United States, however, should not be taken for granted. The recent rise of research universities in other countries may threaten U.S. universities' ability to attract and retain international scholars (Altbach and Balan, 2007). Other countries are competing for individuals to strengthen their research and knowledge production capacities, which increase the importance of the university sector in the economy (United Nations Educational, Scientific and Cultural Organization [UNESCO] Forum for Higher Education, 2008). The U.S. has remained largely immune to this competition, partly due to its confidence with the quality of higher education it provides (NAFSA: Association of International Educators, 2006). Tremewan (2008), however, sends an alarming message to U.S. higher education, forecasting that while the United States had 37 universities in the world's top fifty ranked universities in 2005, the numbers will be significantly decreased to fifteen by 2050.

Higher education institutions in the United States must continue to attract the best and brightest scholars and students from around the world (Bartell, 2003; Johnson, 2000; Olson and Kroeger, 2001). Attracting international faculty and retaining them serve the double purpose of maintaining U.S. competitiveness and educating Americans about the world beyond our borders (McCalman, 2007). In order to keep these scholars and maximize their contribution, researchers need to identify and understand the issues and challenges facing international faculty. More research on international faculty is needed, particularly with regard to their satisfaction and morale. In contrast to research on U.S. faculty, international faculty are less satisfied than their U.S.-born colleagues while being more productive. We currently do not know why this is the case or how it affects international faculty in their daily life or in their views on mobility. More research using other measures of productivity, including those that include teaching and advising as variables, is needed. Finally, given the relatively little research on faculty mobility in general and on international faculty mobility in particular, it is important for institutional researchers to collect more detailed information about how international faculty members move, where they move, and why. It is worth noting that there are essentially four mobility options for international faculty: (1) no mobility (get a faculty job and stay at the same institution), (2) move to another institution within the United States, (3) return to the home country or country of native language, or (4) move out of academe altogether. There are a number of factors that might make international faculty mobility patterns significantly different from those of their native U.S.-born and -educated faculty colleagues. Some of these factors, such as lack of family ties in the United States or the tendency of scientists to work in large national and international collaborative research groups, could promote mobility. Others, such as concerns over immigration and preference for living in certain geographic areas, might promote staying put. Some factors, such as satisfaction or climate, for international faculty could do both. We do not know how or to what extent international faculty mobility is motivated by prestige or salary. These are among the many questions that the data collection and analysis of institutional researchers can help to answer regarding this important sector of the U.S. faculty.

Finally, it is becoming clear that large-scale data sets can take us only so far in understanding the dynamics of noncitizen faculty experiences in higher education as well as mobility patterns and variables that explain them. These national data suggest that there are differences between noncitizen and U.S. faculty with respect to satisfaction and propensity to move to another college or university or out of academe altogether, but they offer somewhat contradictory explanations for this phenomenon. To paraphrase our economist colleague, Donna Ginther, we tortured the data and found that citizenship status matters, but beyond that, the difference in mobility between U.S. and non-U.S. citizen faculty is not captured by the questions being asked in national surveys. Qualitative studies could help to clarify several points about non-U.S. faculty, such as explaining the actual experiences of international faculty and offering insight into issues such as satisfaction, productivity, and mobility.

Implications for institutional researchers are several. First, from an institutional research perspective, how international status is defined matters. Using citizenship masks certain differences, while using birthplace masks others. Faculty members, regardless of place of birth, are more similar if they have undergraduate degrees from U.S. colleges than they are if they were born and educated abroad. Nonresident alien status, as another way of defining international faculty, makes the matter more complicated. Institutional researchers may need to collect data on the various definitions and conduct analyses in different ways to discover important distinctions between international faculty and their domestic counterparts. As we show in our research using national data sets, one needs to be cognizant of the definitions used and how that influences raw numbers as well as their meaning and interpretation.

Second, the data we review in this chapter suggest that institutional researchers need to continuously track who their faculty are, where they come from, what they experience, and, if they leave, where and why they go. This tracking calls for the use of both quantitative and qualitative data. Periodic focus groups and/or interviews with faculty can help the institution better understand the experiences of this important group of faculty. For example, the research cited in this chapter suggests that international faculty are less satisfied with the interaction with their departmental and institutional colleagues, and only qualitative research can help us understand why this is the case and what the institution can do to remedy this problem.

Finally, international faculty is an important constituency group, and their presence and importance are likely to increase over time. However, as a group they are often overlooked and frequently underestimated and misunderstood. When conducting on-campus studies of faculty, regardless of topic, understanding international faculty, however defined, matters. If institutions want to understand faculty life on their campuses, they will have to ask questions in such a way as to reflect similarities or differences among U.S. and international faculty. Institutions must have a good sense of who their international faculty members are, what their needs are, what their experiences are like, and how they are contributing to the academic and social life of the institution.

References

Altbach, P., and Balan, J. *World Class Worldwide: Transforming Research Universities in Asian and Latin America.* Baltimore, Md.: Johns Hopkins University Press, 2007.

Bartell, M. "Internationalization of Universities: A University Culture-Based Framework." *Higher Education,* 2003, *45*(1), 43–70.

Bound, J., Turner, S., and Walsh, P. "Internationalization of U.S. Doctorate Education." NBER Working Paper No. 14792, March 2009.

Corley, E. A., and Sabharwal, M. "Foreign Born Academic Scientists and Engineers: Producing More and Getting Less Than Their U.S. Born Peers?" *Research in Higher Education,* 2007, *48*(8), 909–940.

Ehrenberg, R., Kasper, H., and Rees, D. "Faculty Turnover at American Colleges and Universities: Analyses of AAUP Data." *Economics of Education Review,* 1991, *10*(2), 99–110.

Ehrenberg, R. G., Rizzo, M. J., and Condie, S. S. "Start-up Costs in American Research Universities." Prepared by Cornell Higher Education Research Institute, Cornell University, 2003. (ED 482 445)

Hoffer, T., Hess, M., Welch, V., and Williams, K. "Doctorate Recipients From United States Universities: Summary Report." Retrieved July 22, 2008, from http://www.nsf. gov/statistics/doctorates/pdf/sed2006.pdf.

Johnson, J. M. "International Mobility of Doctoral Recipients from U.S. Universities." Paper presented at Council of Graduate Schools Annual Meeting, New Orleans, La., December, 2000.

Johnsrud, L. K., and Rosser, V. J. "Faculty Members' Morale and Their Intentions to Leave: A Multilevel Explanation." *Journal of Higher Education*, 2002, 73(4), 518–542.

Kerr, W. R., and Lincoln, W. F. "The Supply Side of Innovation: H-1B Visa Reforms and US Ethnic Invention." Harvard Business School Working Paper, 2009. Retrieved January 4, 2012, from http://hbswk.hbs.edu/item/6097.html.

Kim, D. B., Wolf-Wendel, L., and Twombly, S. "Predicting International Faculty Satisfaction and Productivity Using Alternative Definitions and Institutional Characteristics." *Journal of Higher Education*, 2011, 82(6), 720–747.

Levin, S., and Stephan, P. "Are the Foreign Born a Source of Strength for U.S. Science?" *Science*, 1999, 285(5431), 1213–1214.

Levine, D. I., and Strauss, G. "Employee Participation and Involvement." ERIC Document Reproduction Service, 1989. (ED 317 704)

Lowell, B. L. "Skilled Temporary and Permanent Immigrants in the United States." *Population Research and Policy Review*, 2001, 20, 33–58.

Mamiseishvili, K., and Rosser, V. "Examining the Relationship Between Faculty Productivity and Job Satisfaction." *Journal of the Professoriate*, 2011, 5(2), 100–132.

Manrique, C. G., and Manrique, G. G. *The Multicultural or Immigrant Faculty in American Society*. Lewiston, N.Y.: Edwin Mellen Press, 1999.

Marvasti, A. "U.S. Academic Institutions and Perceived Effectiveness of Foreign-Born Faculty." *Journal of Economic Issues*, 2005, 39(1), 151–176.

McCalman, C. L. "Being an Interculturally Competent Instructor in the United States: Issues of Classroom Dynamics and Appropriateness, and Recommendations for International Instructors." *New Directions for Teaching and Learning*, 2007, 101, 65–74.

NAFSA: Association of International Educators. *Restoring U.S. Competitiveness: For International Students and Scholars*. Washington, D.C.: NAFSA, 2006.

Olson, C. L., and Kroeger, K. R. "Global Competency and Intercultural Sensitivity." *Journal of Studies in International Education*, 2001, 5(2), 116–137.

"Open Doors 2008." *Institute for International Education*. Retrieved November 20, 2008, from http://opendoors.iienetwork.org/.

Rosser, V. J. "Faculty Members' Intentions to Leave: A National Study on Their Worklife and Satisfaction." *Research in Higher Education*, 2004, 45(3), 285–309.

Schuster, J., and Finkelstein, M. *The American Faculty*. Baltimore, Md.: Johns Hopkins University Press, 2006.

Skachkova, P. "Academic Careers of Immigrant Women Professors in the U.S." *Higher Education*, 2007, 53, 697–738.

Smart, J. C. "A Causal Model of Faculty Turnover Intentions." *Research in Higher Education*, 1990, 31(5), 405–424.

Theobald, R. *Foreign-Born Early-Career Faculty in American Higher Education*. Dissertation, University of Colorado, Boulder, 2007.

Thomas, J. M., and Johnson, B. J. "Perspectives of International Faculty Members: Their Experiences and Stories." *Education and Society*, 2004, 22(3), 47–64.

Thomas, S. L., and Heck, R. H. "Analysis of Large-Scale Secondary Data in Higher Education Research: Potential Perils Associated With Complex Sampling Designs." *Research in Higher Education*, 2001, 42(5), 517–540.

Tremewan, C. UNESCO Forum Workshop on Postgraduate Education, Dublin, Ireland, 2008.

United Nations Educational, Scientific and Cultural Organization (UNESCO) Forum for Higher Education. "Research and Knowledge: Challenges for Research Systems in the Knowledge Society." Paper presented at the Association for the Study of Higher Education conference, Jacksonville, Fla., November 2008.

Watts, J. R. "The H-1-B Visa: Free Market Solutions for Business and Labor." *Population Research and Policy Review*, 2001, *20*, 143–156.

Wells, R., and others. "Job Satisfaction of International Faculty in U.S. Higher Education." *Journal of the Professoriate*, 2007, *2*, 5–32.

Xu, Y. "Gender Disparity in STEM Disciplines: A Study of Faculty Attrition and Turnover Intentions." *Research in Higher Education*, 2008, *49*, 607–624.

Zhou, Y., and Volkwein, J. "Examining the Influences on Faculty Departure Intentions: A Comparison of Tenured Versus Non-tenured Faculty at Research Universities Using NSOPF-99." *Research in Higher Education*, 2004, *45*(2), 139–176.

DONGBIN KIM *is an associate professor of educational leadership and policy studies at the University of Kansas.*

SUSAN TWOMBLY *is a professor and chair of educational leadership and policy studies at the University of Kansas.*

LISA WOLF-WENDEL *is a professor of educational leadership and policy studies at the University of Kansas.*

3

This chapter describes the characteristics of non-tenure-track faculty, which now make up the majority of faculty on campuses; highlights the importance of reporting complete data; and calls upon institutional researchers to contribute to addressing this growing segment of the faculty.

Missing from the Institutional Data Picture: Non-Tenure-Track Faculty

Adrianna Kezar, Daniel Maxey

Institutional researchers might know more about non-tenure-track (NTT) faculty[1] than leaders on many college campuses, particularly four-year institutions and research universities (Cross and Goldenberg, 2009). As such, institutional researchers play an important role in educating campus leaders about this growing segment of the academic workforce. Gappa and Leslie (1993) first identified a trend for these faculty to be ignored by administrators, tenured and tenure-track faculty, and staff, and labeled NTT faculty the "invisible faculty." Times are changing; with two-thirds of the faculty now off the tenure track across higher education, it is hard to ignore the new majority. Yet many campuses have few, if any, processes in place for identifying, documenting, and creating meaningful policies and practices for this population of faculty.

In this chapter we argue for creating better data about the new faculty majority and also better models for understanding its implications. We first provide an overview of who is included in our definition of NTT faculty and provide some background characteristics about this group. Second, we describe some of the reasons why it is important to obtain reliable data on this group beyond just their rising numbers. Third, we describe some of the reasons why it has been difficult to obtain complete data on NTT faculty. Finally, we focus on recommendations for institutional researchers about ways they might go about collecting reliable, effective, and helpful data to inform campus policymaking.

NEW DIRECTIONS FOR INSTITUTIONAL RESEARCH, no. 155, Fall 2012 © Wiley Periodicals, Inc.
Published online in Wiley Online Library (wileyonlinelibrary.com) • DOI: 10.1002/ir.20021

Overview of NTT Faculty Nationally

Over the past several decades, the faculties of U.S. institutions of higher education have come to be composed mostly of individuals who are off the tenure track. The volume of research conducted on this issue suggests that this growth has not gone completely unnoticed (Baldwin and Chronister, 2001; Gappa and Leslie, 1993; Kezar and Sam, 2010a, 2010b; Schuster and Finkelstein, 2006). However, much is still not understood about the NTT faculty who now make up two-thirds of the faculty in postsecondary education. Incomplete data on NTT faculty is a problem at the national and institutional level. Working toward filling gaps in the research and establishing mechanisms to ensure the accurate collection of data regarding NTT faculty should be a priority for institutional researchers as we seek to understand how growth in this sector has fostered inequities in the academic workforce, altered or bypassed traditional compensation and promotion models, and affected student learning.

The term *NTT faculty* commonly denotes both full- and part-time academic staff that are not on the tenure track. Data from the 2007 Integrated Postsecondary Education Data System (IPEDS) survey shows that 66 percent of all faculty at nonprofit institutions were employed off the tenure track and approximately 47 percent of all faculty held part-time positions (American Federation of Teachers [AFT], 2009). A report produced by the AFT (2009) compares data collected through the IPEDS survey over the decade between 1997 and 2007 and calls attention to the pace of change in the composition of the faculty. According to the IPEDS data analyzed in the report, over the span of ten years the proportion of NTT faculty among the professoriate increased significantly, contrasted by a decrease in the percentage of tenured and tenure-track faculty. In 1997, tenured and tenure-track faculty accounted for 40.7 percent of the faculty. By 2007, the proportion of tenured and tenure-track faculty had declined by about 6 percent to 34.5 percent. However, the proportion of full-time NTT faculty increased from 17.4 percent to 18.8 percent, and part-time faculty increased from 41.9 percent to 46.7 percent.

Discussing these changes in terms of proportions helps to demonstrate the shift in faculty positions from the tenure track to NTT positions. Considering the rate of growth among each category emphasizes this point and underscores the significantly increased reliance on full- and part-time NTT faculty. Between 1997 and 2007, tenure-track positions increased by 34,109 or 8.6 percent; full-time NTT positions grew by 64,733 or 38.2 percent; and part-time positions grew by 173,529 or 42.6 percent (AFT, 2009). The data included in the AFT report do not include for-profit institutions wherein the faculty is composed entirely of NTT positions. Including data from this growing segment of postsecondary education would increase the numbers and proportions of NTT positions in higher education significantly. Also, while this chapter focuses on faculty positions, it is important to note that the number of graduate assistants, many of whom serve in instructional roles, also increased significantly. The AFT report shows a 48.5 percent increase in the number of graduate assistants between 1997 and 2007.

Part-Time Faculty. Part-time faculty have experienced the most substantial rate of growth over the past forty years. The number of part-time faculty employed increased by 422.1 percent between 1970 and 2003, compared to an increase of only 70.7 percent among all full-time faculty, both tenure-track and NTT (Schuster and Finkelstein, 2006). While discussions often characterize part-time faculty as one homogeneous class of employees, they are actually a very heterogeneous group with no common profile, motivation, or contract. Gappa and Leslie (1993) attempted to create a typology so that campus leaders could understand this population. They identified four broad categories: (1) career enders; (2) specialists, experts, and professionals; (3) aspiring academics; and (4) freelancers. *Career-enders* are people who are retired or in the process of retiring. They may be faculty who decided to teach in retirement, or they may come from established careers outside of academia. *Specialists, experts, and professionals* are faculty who are employed full-time elsewhere, and come from a varied range of careers. They are hired for their specialized knowledge or success in certain fields, be it the arts or business. Often these individuals do not rely on the faculty positions for income but enjoy being involved in the academy and teaching. *Aspiring academics* are faculty members who are looking for a full-time or tenure-track position. So-called "freeway fliers" are a type of aspiring academic that typically teach at multiple institutions to create the equivalent of a full-time position (Gappa and Leslie, 1993). *Freelancers* typically have a job outside of academe and supplement their income with teaching. Some are also caretakers at home and prefer the flexibility of working part-time because of other demands.

Part-time faculty have long been a part of higher education, particularly within the community college sector, where they grew in numbers beginning in the 1970s. However, they were not commonly represented in large numbers across four-year institutions and research universities until the past decade or so. In 1993, community colleges averaged 60 percent part-time faculty (Gappa and Leslie, 1993). More recently, this percentage at some schools has actually been found to be as high as 80 percent (AFT, 2003; National Education Association, 2007). The research and doctorate-granting universities have begun to follow the employment patterns of community colleges, with an increasing number of the new faculty hires being part-time and off the tenure track. There has been a recent increase in the use of part-time faculty at all institutions (AFT, 2009). Community colleges have increased their part-time faculty population from approximately 66 percent to 69 percent. Public comprehensive institutions have seen approximate growth of part-time faculty from 36 percent to 46 percent. Public research institutions saw proportions rise from about 23 percent to 27 percent, although this sector also experienced a rate of growth in graduate assistants that is higher than what has been observed among other types of institutions. Proportions of part-time faculty at private nonprofit research and comprehensive institutions increased approximately 4 percent and 10 percent, respectively (AFT, 2009).

These overall numbers are not uniform throughout the departments. Both community colleges and four-year research/doctoral/comprehensive institutions saw high percentages of part-time faculty in composition and humanities courses, as well as math and science courses. According to a report by the National Education Association (NEA, 2007), the highest increases in part-time faculty occurred in the humanities, social sciences, and agriculture, and the greatest increase from 1987 to 2003 being in education.[2] While part-time positions have increased, rising numbers of full-time NTT positions also have significant implications for institutions.

Full-Time NTT Faculty. Whereas part-time faculty might teach at more than one institution, full-time NTT faculty are typically employed at a single institution. In 1969, full-time NTT faculty made up about 3 percent of the faculty (Schuster and Finkelstein, 2006). By 2007, these faculty members accounted for 18.8 percent of faculty positions on campuses nationwide (AFT, 2009). Baldwin and Chronister (2001) established a typology to better understand full-time NTT faculty based on the terms of their employment responsibilities: teachers, researchers, administrators, and other academic professionals. *Teachers* are those who spend over two-thirds of their time in instruction, with the rest of their time split between administrative tasks and research. *Researchers* are those specifically hired to conduct research for over half their time, dividing the other half between instruction and administration. *Administrators* are those who spend about half their time in administrative work (for example, an associate dean) and the rest of the time in research and other activities. The final group is composed of other *academic professionals*. These full-time NTT faculty spend half of their time with activities other than teaching, research, or administration. They are often lab technicians, programmers, or community service members. Usually, they spend a quarter of their time teaching, depending on their qualifications (Baldwin and Chronister, 2001).

Full-time NTT positions have been increasing over time, particularly at four-year institutions. Schuster and Finkelstein (2006) note that full-time NTT faculty comprised a majority of all new full-time hires, outpacing tenure-track positions, in 1993. The authors indicate that by 2003, 58.6 percent of new full-time faculty positions were hired off the tenure track. Much like part-time faculty, the proportion of full-time faculty varies by institutional type. According to 2007 IPEDS data (AFT, 2009), full-time NTT positions accounted for 13 percent to 14 percent of the faculty at the community colleges; at public and private comprehensive institutions, approximately 11 percent and 18 percent, respectively; and among public and private research institutions, 24 percent and 23 percent, respectively. The study showed that, overall, it seems that the proportion of full-time NTT positions has remained somewhat constant over the past decade.

While full-time NTT positions were somewhat stable, the other categories have seen more or less consistent increases or decreases; the part-time faculty are increasing in proportion, the share of tenured and tenure-track appointments is decreasing, and graduate assistants are increasing in some sectors, although their roles are not fully understood. In other words, there is steady growth of NTT faculty positions as a proportion of the professoriate. This background is meant to help readers understand the basic differences between part-time and full-time NTT designations, as well as their placement across different institutional types. It is important to note that NTT faculty are an extremely heterogeneous group with different motivations, experiences, and backgrounds. This heterogeneity will likely become a challenge in data collection, disaggregation, and reporting.

Why Do We Need Reliable Data?

Some may be convinced that the sheer number and growth of these faculty on campuses is reason enough that we should have accurate data about their numbers, rehire, salary, benefits, and promotion (where applicable). One of the main reasons for collecting data on tenure-track faculty is to be able to identify inequities and trends that are relevant for policymaking. Some data already indicate that problems exist among NTT faculty related to equity and policymaking, suggesting the need for more data and a more purposeful examination of these issues. Other data suggest inconsistencies with regard to compensation and promotion standards and negative impacts on student outcomes produced by NTT faculty working conditions. Resolving each of these issues is going to require additional, more complete data at the institutional and national level.

Potential Violation of Affirmative Action. Several scholars have pointed to the fact that institutions usually do not hire NTT faculty systematically and have violated equal opportunity for employment regulations (Gappa and Leslie, 1993; Hollenshead and others, 2007). There has been a concerted effort to make higher education more accountable for hiring a diverse workforce. Yet the lack of systematic hiring for NTT faculty may prove counter to these carefully planned efforts, threatening advances made among tenure-track faculty and creating new inequalities. Over the years, women have been hired disproportionately for NTT jobs. As a result, they are underrepresented in tenure-track jobs in comparison to their percentage or availability of graduating doctoral candidates. Schuster and Finkelstein (2006) noted that women were twice as likely as men to be off the tenure track. Harper, Baldwin, Gansneder, and Chronister (2001) note that there is a disproportionate growth in number and proportion of women in full-time NTT positions. Harper and others found that in the case of faculty rank for NTT faculty, women were least likely to move to the highest available position.

For racial and ethnic minorities, the overall trend leans slightly toward racial and ethnic minorities being overrepresented in NTT faculty positions. Schuster and Finkelstein (2006) reported that Asian faculty were 7.3 percent, other nonwhite faculty were 9.8 percent, while white faculty were 82.9 percent of the full-time NTT faculty. Baldwin and Chronister (2001) note that faculty of color in full-time NTT appointments increased by 87 percent, while experiencing only a 40 percent increase in the tenure-line positions.

With regard to part-time faculty, the numbers seem to be a little different from the full-time NTT sector. Gappa and Leslie (1993) found that only 9.2 percent of the part-time faculty were ethnic or racial minorities. They raised concerns at the apparent lack of diversity in part-time appointments. The 2009 AFT study found that among the part-time hires, black faculty increased by 0.5 percent, Asian/Pacific Islander faculty increased by 0.2 percent, Hispanic faculty increased by 0.4 percent, and Native Americans showed little increase. In 2007, the percentage of ethnic minorities among part-time faculty was still at 9 percent (AFT, 2009). It appears that the part-time faculty lack diversity proportional to their numbers in the hiring pool and compared to whites.

Salary, Benefits, and Promotion. Across a variety of studies, a major concern noted by NTT faculty is the inconsistency in the application of policies. Hollenshead and others (2007) conducted a national survey that suggests there are typically no institutional standards as it relates to salary, benefits, and promotion of contingent faculty members. Many institutions allow individual units to create policies regarding all of these issues, and there may be incredible variation, for example, with salary. Gappa and Leslie (1993) describe a multitude of policies for part-time faculty that are inconsistently applied within institutions: hiring processes, contract terms, salary, participation in governance, evaluation, promotion, and a host of other working conditions that vary from department to department and sometimes even from person to person, which raises concerns about equity. Baldwin and Chronister (2001) describe the situation where full-time NTT faculty members on three- and five-year contracts had their appointments changed to one-year contracts when a new department chair took control. Due to the lack of standards or set policies, policies can be changed on a whim.

Student Learning. While equity is important and we hope that the academic workplace provides fair conditions, the underlying goal of higher education institutions is to foster student learning. However, it appears that the lack of systemic planning around NTT faculty working conditions is creating a workplace that negatively shapes student learning. Some studies have demonstrated that NTT faculty working conditions

NEW DIRECTIONS FOR INSTITUTIONAL RESEARCH • DOI: 10.1002/ir

shape job performance, which likely affects student learning (Kezar, 2012). For example, Ehrenberg and Zhang (2005) examined institutions with large numbers of NTT faculty and compared them to institutions that utilize fewer. The findings identified lower graduation rates at institutions that used greater proportions of NTT faculty in instruction. Bettinger and Long (2004) found that students who take courses with adjuncts tend to receive higher grades and have interest in taking further courses. However, they also found that taking more courses with adjunct professors results in lower graduation rates. Carrell and West (2010) found that students who take courses with adjuncts perform significantly worse in follow-up courses compared to students that started out taking courses with tenured or tenure-track faculty. Eagan and Jaeger (2009) and Jaeger and Eagan (2009) found that increasing exposure to part-time faculty in the community college sector, in other words, taking more courses with them, negatively affected the likelihood that students would transfer to four-year institutions. Why might exposure to NTT faculty lead to less desirable student outcomes? Studies that document their working conditions suggest reasons for the less desirable outcome. NTT faculty are often assigned to teach classes at the last minute, are provided no professional development, and are not informed of the learning goals for the department or college. They are unsure about continuous employment and are unlikely to update their course materials because of the instability. Additionally, they frequently lack access to basic materials and resources needed for teaching. Unless we collect data about NTT faculty working conditions, we will be unable to improve the learning environment for students, and decision makers will remain largely unaware of problems that exist.

Why Are Reliable Data Incomplete?

There is a dearth of information exploring why reliable data on NTT faculty are incomplete, but existing research points to a combination of structural and political factors. In their study of 10 elite research institutions, Cross and Goldenberg (2009) identified several structural factors that led these campuses to have no, little, or poor data about NTT faculty. Among the factors they identified are a lack of uniformity with regard to titles, decentralization of hiring, and inconsistent standards and policies for departments reporting data to the institution. A number of political factors tied to a lack of commitment to addressing issues related to the presence and growth of NTT faculty on college campuses also exist.

Different Titles. Titles and basic responsibilities for tenured and tenure-track positions are mostly uniform across the country. The titles full professor, associate, and assistant professor generally carry the same meaning from one institution to another and within a campus (Cross and Goldenberg, 2009; Shavers, 2000). Whereas distinctions between tenure-track positions are common throughout postsecondary education in this country, no standard framework of job titles exists to define common work responsibilities or types of appointment for NTT faculty. We presented some of the challenges associated with trying to understand NTT faculty as a group, given their heterogeneity, in the overview. While the typologies articulated by Gappa and Leslie (1993) and Baldwin and Chronister (2001) help researchers begin to differentiate NTT faculty and their experiences, these typologies do not typically align with actual job titles in the workplace. Variation among titles for both full- and part-time NTT faculty can be significant. For example, Berry (2005) lists fifty various titles and terms given to part-time faculty alone, providing examples such as *casual*, *sessional*, or *adjunct* professors.[3] The absence of common titles complicates comparisons between institutions, masks distinctions between contractual relationships between faculty and the institution, and makes it increasingly difficult to follow trends related to NTT faculty nationwide. The wide variation also masks distinctions among opportunities for reappointment or promotion, seniority, job focus, and contract terms. Studies have demonstrated it is often just as difficult to produce an accurate accounting of NTT faculty in a single institution as well as within an entire system (Cross and Goldenberg, 2009).

In much the same way as they differ across institutions, NTT faculty titles even differ within individual institutions, making the collection of data extremely difficult for institutional researchers (Cross and Goldenberg, 2009; Kezar and Sam, 2010b). In fact, on many campuses, colleges and departments create their own distinct titles. Even when titles appear to be somewhat similar between departments, the job duties assigned by different units may vary significantly, sometimes masking distinctions between faculty positions. The Cross and Goldenberg (2009) study confirmed prior findings of a wide range of titles across and within institutions. The authors also found that campuses used certain titles to denote NTT faculty, regardless of their full- or part-time status, masking differences between the two. The title *lecturer* at one campus may indicate a part-time faculty member, while another campus might use this term for a full-time NTT position. A different department or campus may use the term *instructor* for a faculty member with the same work responsibilities. Similarly, in a single campus, the meaning and responsibilities of *clinical faculty* may be different depending on department or school. Often, confusion over titles masks differences between types of NTT faculty. Deans and department chairs at the institutions studied by Cross and Goldenberg (2009) have been found to use broad terms like *academic professionals* to describe all NTT faculty, not understanding that most of these instructors do not carry certain privileges afforded to that particular employment classification, such as one-year notice rights (Cross and Goldenberg, 2009). Casual use of terms like *instructor* or *lecturer* also produces confusion when those terms do not correspond to actual appointment status or records maintained by either human resources or institutional researchers.

Some states have sought to bring some degree of uniformity to title designations in their higher education systems. For example, New Hampshire makes a distinction between tenure-track and NTT positions through the use of the terms *status* and *nonstatus appointments* in institutions' human resources systems (Kezar and Sam, 2010b). Still, in many higher education systems, similar titles may signify different positions. For example, the term *fixed-term* may indicate a full-time NTT faculty member on one campus and a part-time faculty member on another campus. Such a lack of uniformity with regard to job titles contributes to inconsistencies and inaccuracies in data that departments report to institutions or, at the very least, complicates interpretation of the data by researchers.

Decentralization of Hiring. The decentralized nature of hiring leads to the proliferation of titles as various disciplines have developed different conventions. As responsibility-centered management and other decentralized management models have become more common on campuses, many budgetary decisions and processes including hiring have moved from the institution to the college and department levels (Cross and Goldenberg, 2009). Decentralization has redistributed responsibility for decision making to a larger number of individuals across multiple colleges and departments within an institution. As a result, more individuals are responsible for making staffing decisions, particularly regarding NTT faculty, than in the past. At this level, decisions to hire NTT faculty are often made casually, without regard for institutional standards, and with little input from faculty or the administration.

While institutions typically have clearly defined procedures in place for filling tenure-track positions, NTT hiring is often conducted without formal guidelines. Vacant tenure-track positions are often filled by conducting national searches wherein rigid screening and selection processes are followed to determine who will fill a limited number of tenure-track positions on campus. Colleges and departments often lack formal procedures for recruiting and hiring NTT faculty and approach these tasks casually, particularly when part-time faculty are hired (Cross and Goldenberg, 2009; Gappa and Leslie, 1993). Research by Hollenshead and others (2007) suggests that trends may be shifting toward a more structured approach for hiring full-time NTT faculty. In any event, institutions usually lack limits on the number of NTT faculty that can be employed. As a result of the lack of guidelines and standards, or at least any guarantee that existing standards are adhered to, hiring practices for NTT faculty are inconsistent. While tenure-track positions are usually filled through exhaustive, national searches, NTT faculty, especially part-time faculty, are often hired locally by departments and on a semester basis, as dictated by the demands of the moment (Kezar and Sam, 2010b).

Departmental decisions to hire faculty off the tenure track usually are not the direct result of mandates from senior administrators at the institution (Cross and Goldenberg, 2009). Rather, presidents, provosts, and governing boards are typically unaware of just how many NTT positions exist on their campuses and how their rise has affected outcomes for student learning. Senior administrators unwittingly and indirectly influence these decisions, however, since the choice to hire faculty is strongly influenced by department budgets and enrollments. As Cross and Goldenberg (2009) point out, the decentralization of hiring produces significant cause for concern, but more troublesome is the fact that no one at the institutional level seems to be monitoring or controlling these practices to control the inevitable outcomes of the unchecked growth of NTT faculty.

Reporting from Departments and Schools. The constantly changing and decentralized nature of NTT hiring practices and wide-ranging job titles at an institution creates a perplexing problem for institutional researchers. Disparate titles and variance in hiring processes can make it very difficult for institutional research offices to pinpoint the exact number of faculty employed at a given time, identify trends in hiring, and determine how many students are receiving instruction from NTT faculty. Information management systems and human resources databases at the institutional level might not capture all data since some information is primarily collected and maintained at the department level. None of the institutions in the Cross and Goldenberg (2009) study could produce accurate data related to the number of faculty employed and the courses they teach. This is, in part, due to the complicated task described earlier, but also because individual departments often maintain their own systems and report inaccurate or incomplete data to their institutions.

Because departments are often responsible for maintaining some information about NTT faculty in a manner that is disconnected from other information, making meaning from data that do exist is complicated by the fact that much of the information collected is managed in decentralized systems and in different offices within the university or college. For example, departments might be responsible for maintaining teaching data, while personnel records that include information like tenure status might be managed by human resources. Anyone trying to determine who teaches which courses or how many students receive instruction from NTT faculty is going to face difficulty trying to draw that information out. At the department level, Cross and Goldenberg (2009) also demonstrate that staff often subscribe to different philosophies about which records should be maintained. Their study revealed that individual departments were not always diligent about maintaining accurate and complete records related to their employment and use of NTT faculty. Inaccurate and unreliable data kept at the department level create challenges associated with understanding the profile of NTT faculty, particularly since institutions do not always have the means to accurately interpret and report data provided by departments and schools. In fact, a result of these inconsistencies is that deans and more senior administrators on campuses are often not sure of the composition of the faculty or the number of part- and full-time

NTT faculty employed in any part of the institution or the whole (Cross and Goldenberg, 2009).

The low level of detail maintained by some departments must certainly create many frustrations for institutional researchers, complicating an already difficult task of providing a clear picture of the faculty. It is important to stress that these challenges for receiving and maintaining data are not the fault of institutional researchers but the product of decentralization within institutions. However, solving the problem may not be as easy as getting stakeholders together to connect systems, creating one management system for all data. Not only are systems not always connected, but units across an institution may not record data in a manner that is conducive to merging disparate systems into one. Even where strong information management systems exist, relying on data reported by departments and attempting to make comparisons of data from different sources can complicate the work of institutional researchers. Cross and Goldenberg (2009) note that many institutions are beginning to take charge of management systems and creating standards for data reporting from individual units, although such examples are recent developments. Nonetheless, efforts to streamline data reporting and management will significantly contribute to efforts to reform practice related to NTT faculty.

The implications for this data reporting reach well beyond the campus boundaries. Inaccurate or incomplete data are transmitted to external stakeholders including the U.S. Department of Education, state officials, accrediting agencies, and others and included in reports and studies as though they were factual representations (Cross and Goldenberg, 2009). Some believe that existing reports on the number of NTT faculty employed across higher education are significantly underestimated as a result.

Lack of Prioritization. While Cross and Goldenberg (2009) focus on three key elements for why campuses have poor data about NTT faculty, based on case studies one author of the chapter has conducted and a national interview study done on NTT faculty leaders, we have identified two other factors that appear to influence this process. Institutional leaders, including members of governing boards, presidents, and provosts, do not make data collection of NTT faculty a priority. They have not asked institutional researchers to standardize titles or to create processes to obtain better data from departments, and have not asked for the data themselves about NTT faculty. Even when institutional leaders oppose increased reliance on NTT faculty, these priorities are not always transmitted to other campus decision makers and staff (Cross and Goldenberg, 2009). Clearly, if institutional researchers and campus staff are not asked for data about this population, they would be unlikely to collect and monitor. For accurate data to be created it needs to be a priority among campus leaders.

Fear of Unionization. A second reason for a lack of data collection is not a lack of priority by leaders, but fear that the collection of such data could lead to unionization on their campus and unwillingness by those leaders to engage in collective bargaining. Data collection is often used as a part of making the case for collective bargaining because salary inequities, lack of benefits, and problematic policies are brought to light. National unions have often used comparative data to demonstrate to faculty that their administration is not being equitable or treating them fairly and that they need another party to intervene to create appropriate working conditions. Even private campuses that were once shielded from collective bargaining are now worried about unions coming to their campuses because many recent court cases demonstrate that the faculty, particularly contingent faculty, are not managers and do not participate in decision making, so they are eligible for collective bargaining.

We bring up these last two reasons why reliable data are not available to illustrate that while structural issues are at play, there are also leadership and political issues that institutional researchers will need to navigate as they begin to help campuses obtain needed data to create better campus policy and ultimately enhance student learning.

What Can Institutional Researchers Do?

There are a variety of practices in which institutional researchers can engage that will benefit institutions and provide leadership on the issue of making NTT faculty successful, which can lead to improved student learning. Institutional researchers can contribute to constructing policies and fostering priorities to produce more reliable data across their institutions. Researchers should also be attentive to reports and recommendations issued by national organizations to remain informed about efforts under way elsewhere.

Develop a Rubric of Standard Titles. Tenure-track faculty have standard titles that are used across most institutions. There is no reason why standard titles cannot be created for NTT faculty as well. Yet this will be a complex task as the overview of NTT faculty noted the heterogeneity of this group of faculty. It is important that NTT faculty be brought into discussions about titles because many of the existing titles have very negative inferences. Titles often speak to what faculty are not, such as NTT or contingent, rather than what they are, instructors or lecturers. NTT faculty should have the opportunity to work with others on campus to create titles that they feel represent their work and profession. At the same time as we need to respect NTT faculty voice, campuses should consider that their data goes to state and federal sources, so looking to external groups for ideas may help with the macro standardization goal. It is advisable that institutional researchers be a member of an ad hoc committee that is established with representative members from departments and units across the university or college. Also, it might help to look at some of the titles that have been created within unionized campuses that have addressed this issue or state systems that have created standardized language. State systems that have standardized language might also benefit from revisiting the titles they have to be sure that they encapsulate the heterogeneity of NTT faculty.

Look Beyond Titles for Contractual Distinctions. Although titles are important, institutional researchers should be mindful that titles often mask contractual differences among NTT faculty. Examining different characteristics of full- and part-time contracts is necessary to develop a more complete understanding of the faculty. Contract terms and job responsibilities may vary as significantly as titles within a system or campus, subjecting individuals with seemingly similar appointments to different employment terms and job responsibilities. Factors such as reappointment and renewal terms, probationary periods, promotion tracks, salary, and seniority policies often differ and may be influenced by the presence and coverage of collective bargaining agreements on campus. Understanding that differences exist among these factors and ensuring their consideration with other data will bring an added dimension of recognition of NTT faculty roles to campus discussions and inform policy development. For example, institutional researchers should consider trends regarding the length of appointment and conditions for reappointment. While some faculty contracts provide multiyear appointments, others, particularly part-time faculty, might be hired on a semester basis with limited, if any, assurance of reappointment.

Collect Not Just Numbers but Information About Policy and Experiences. While institutional researchers typically focus on numerical data, campuses would benefit from evaluating qualitative data gathered through occasional campus climate surveys to examine the working conditions and job experiences of NTT faculty and identify the change over time. We noted earlier how the poor working conditions of NTT faculty are resulting in negative outcomes for students. Working conditions will not improve on campuses unless NTT faculty are asked about standard issues that might affect their performance such as availability of equipment and resources or lack of availability of professional development. The following policies should be examined: recruitment practices, hiring practices, orientation, availability of office space, access to materials and resources, adequate equipment, availability of secretarial or administrative support, professional development, participation in governance, academic freedom, evaluation and promotion processes, and mentoring. Even as new policies are put in place, it is important that policies are followed up on to see if they work as intended. Campuses that have made significant progress on improving the working conditions for NTT faculty make a commitment to survey their faculty every two to three years to examine the climate as well as existing policies (Kezar and Sam, 2012).

Disaggregate Data for More Accurate Reporting and Analysis. Collecting information about the experiences of NTT faculty is a necessary step toward giving these faculty greater visibility on campus and creating policies better suited for fostering their success and, by extension, the success of students. However, many of the early studies of NTT faculty were difficult to interpret or use because they did not disaggregate data. Minding the heterogeneity of NTT faculty, institutional researchers should strive to further disaggregate data that are collected and reported, lending to a more complete evaluation of the different motivations, levels of satisfaction, compensation and promotion, experience, and impacts that NTT faculty have on their campuses. Disaggregation will help researchers and policymakers to identify differences in how various types of NTT faculty operate on campus, how policies unevenly address their needs and concerns, and ideally will contribute to changes in practice as visibility increases. If institutions can use the typologies noted in the overview as a guide, they can report more meaningful data when conducting climate studies as we have recommended, for example.

Create Mechanisms to Obtain Data Accurately from Departments and Schools. Regardless of whether a decentralized or centralized decision-making process is followed on campus, institutional researchers need to create a mechanism so that information produced at the department, school, and institutional level is reported regularly and in a manner that makes standardized data about NTT faculty members available across an assortment of categories. For example, hiring and rehiring data, length of contract, work profile (number of courses; allotment of role between teaching, service, research, and administration), salary, and benefits should be standard in easily accessed information. Institutional researchers should also establish a system for monitoring campus policies related to NTT faculty and perhaps annually collect information about policies that can be compared and shared with units. Institutional researchers might also reinforce the importance of faculty handbooks and policies including NTT faculty and use data they have collected as benchmarks for creating language for handbooks.

Manage and Help Create a Sense of Priorities About Data Collection. Institutional researchers may find themselves having to take a lead on campus in creating a sense of urgency to collect data on NTT faculty. Senior administrators are overwhelmed with many different priorities ranging from declining state budget allocations to poorly performing endowments, falling graduation rates, and other issues that are likely to take priority. However, institutional researchers can align data collection on NTT faculty to other strategic priorities that campus leaders are focused on. For instance, the poor working conditions of NTT faculty have been associated with lower graduation rates, and by addressing the working conditions of NTT faculty, institutional researchers can help institutions with their goals around graduation.

Create Accountability Systems Around Hiring and Policies. Institutions are encouraged to develop a committee that monitors data about NTT hiring and policies. Some campuses may decide to establish two separate committees, as the groups needed for these two issues and their composition may differ. For issues related to hiring, the committee should create mechanisms to ensure that equal opportunity employment laws are being followed within hiring processes. Institutional researchers may contribute to such efforts if they are involved in collecting data around hiring. As noted earlier, a major problem within institutions where policies exist is that they are not necessarily followed by departments and schools. Institutional researchers can play a key role in monitoring such efforts by regularly surveying units about implementation of policies as well as conducting climate studies, as already noted. The key factor to accountability is that data are not just collected but reviewed by a standing committee that is tasked with informing the administration of problems to address or look into. The committee should also annually review certain standard data on hiring to ensure compliance with federal regulations.

Become Familiar with National Reports and Policy Recommendations. A number of national organizations such as the American Federation of Teachers (2002, 2003, 2008, 2009), National Education Association (2002, 2004, 2007), American Association of University Professors (2003), and Association of American Universities (2001) have issued reports and policy recommendations for reforming institutions' increasing reliance on NTT faculty. These organizations, particularly the unions, have focused on strategies to control the rising proportion of faculty employed off the tenure track and create better conditions for NTT faculty on campuses (Kezar and Sam, 2010a). Institutional researchers should familiarize themselves with these reports, which often contain detailed analysis of trends and suggest questions to further understand the characteristics of NTT faculty and their impact on student learning. Following national reports will help researchers spot trends and make contributions to policy development on their campuses. We have chosen to highlight two reports here. The other reports and policy recommendations listed above are included in the reference list at the end of the chapter.

American Federation of Teachers (2009). American Academic: The State of the Higher Education Workforce 1997–2007. The AFT report, which we have referenced throughout the chapter, made significant contributions to the visibility of NTT faculty, exposing more recent developments in the trending growth among the largest segment of the academic workforce. Comparing Integrated Postsecondary Education Data System (IPEDS) data between 1997 and 2007, the report demonstrated sharp increases in full- and part-time NTT faculty and graduate students serving in instructional roles compared to tenured and tenure-track positions. The data-rich report provides comparison data for different institutional types, demonstrating increased use of NTT faculty across the board, although proportions vary. AFT has made this information available online, where users can view institution-specific data.

National Education Association (2004). The NEA and Contingent Academic Workers in Higher Education: NBI 2004–60 Action Plan. The NEA report recommends targeted action to address and limit growth in the number of contingent, or NTT, faculty in the workforce. While the report places significant emphasis on organizing and collective bargaining strategies to achieve parity for NTT faculty, it also emphasizes the need for additional research and data. The report includes several key questions intended to fill gaps in existing knowledge that are useful for institutional researchers to consider for data collection. For example, trends are discussed and questions are posed to illuminate the number of courses taught, the types of credentials held by instructors, and the use of NTT faculty members in the instruction of online courses. The report also details strategies for political advocacy, leadership development, and communication between tenured, tenure-track, and NTT faculty on campus. Institutional researchers may find these strategies at work on their campuses and should understand their impact on policy and the changing composition of the academic workforce.

Follow Current National Efforts at Data Collection and Report Trends to Campus Constituents. The National Study of Postsecondary Faculty (NSOPF), sponsored by the National Center for Education Statistics, has served as one of the most comprehensive studies of higher education faculty. The study is the only national data set to provide comparative data about faculty across institutions. More recently, NSOPF started collecting data on NTT faculty. However, NSOPF has been discontinued and there is no national source of data to compare and understand broader trends about NTT faculty. Fortunately, a number of organizations representing the interests of NTT faculty have come forward to help fill the void created by the end of NSOPF.

Among them, the Coalition on the Academic Workforce (CAW, n.d.) is a partnership among more than twenty higher education professional associations, disciplinary organizations, and faculty groups founded in 1997 to address issues related to faculty working conditions and their effects on student outcomes.[4] The organization has created a nationwide survey of part- and full-time NTT faculty, graduate teaching assistants, researchers, and postdoctoral fellows. The first survey was conducted in 2010 and examines working conditions, experiences, satisfaction, and attitudes. Usable responses are reported to have been collected from more than 25,000 individuals, representing the largest number of NTT faculty to participate in any such study to date. The results of the study are now available and will contribute to a growing awareness of issues related to NTT faculty in the workplace. The data should be extremely helpful for informing institutional policy, as well.

Another national group, New Faculty Majority (NFM, n.d.), has also started collecting information on NTT faculty.[5] The organization exists to promote professional equity and improved working conditions, and secure academic freedom for NTT faculty. In 2011, NFM conducted a survey as part of a multifaceted study collecting information on teaching and hiring conditions. The data amassed by NFM will be used to advance the goals of this national organization to improve the working conditions for NTT faculty. The results of the NFM and CAW studies will also increase available data on NTT faculty that will help institutional leaders and policymakers make informed decisions about a largely misunderstood and heterogeneous group of individuals that has come to comprise the majority of faculty in American higher education.

There is consensus that we need reliable and ongoing data about NTT faculty to help improve the working conditions, performance, and ultimately the learning environment for students. It is not surprising that the NTT faculty themselves have taken leadership for collecting this data in the absence of a broader effort because they know the power of data to help alert people to problems, to guide better action, and to help organizations learn and grow.

Conclusion

This chapter has demonstrated how lack of reliable and comprehensive data on NTT faculty hiring and policies has led to a breakdown of effectiveness within higher education. Certainly, institutional researchers are not to blame; it is a systemic failure of the academy. However, institutional researchers have an important role in helping campus leaders to understand this growing segment of the academic workforce. Knowing that data are critical to driving policy changes and facilitating effective employment approaches, researchers can contribute to making a significant difference in the work conditions of NTT faculty as one of the most important issues related to student learning and institutional effectiveness. We hope that institutional researchers will take up our call for action and utilize our recommendations for an improved academy.

Notes

1. We will use the terms *non-tenure-track* and *contingent* to refer broadly to all faculty off the tenure track. We will also speak of part-time and full-time faculty that are different contract types within the non-tenure-track category.
2. None of these statistics take into account for-profit institutions where all of the faculty are employed off the tenure track, which also leads to the rise in numbers across higher education.
3. For a complete list of both full-time/tenure-line and part-time faculty, please see Berry (2005, p. XI).
4. More information on the Coalition on the Academic Workforce is available at www.academicworkforce.org/.
5. Additional information on New Faculty Majority is available at www.newfacultymajority.info/national/.

References

American Association of University Professors. *Policy Statement: Contingent Appointments and the Academic Profession*. Washington, D.C.: American Association of University Professors, 2003. Retrieved December 7, 2011, from www.aaup.org/AAUP/pubsres/policydocs/contents/conting-stmt.htm.

American Federation of Teachers (AFT). "Marching Towards Equity: Curbing the Exploitation and Overuse of Part-time and Non-tenured Faculty," 2002. Retrieved November 13, 2011, from www.aft.org/pdfs/highered/marchingequity1001.pdf.

American Federation of Teachers (AFT). *Full-Time Non-Tenure-Track Faculty Report*. Washington, D.C.: American Federation of Teachers, 2003.

American Federation of Teachers (AFT). "AFT Resolution Faculty and College Excellence Campaign," 2008. Retrieved October 15, 2009, from www.aft.org/about/resolution_detail.cfm?articleid=1495.

American Federation of Teachers (AFT). *The American Academic: The State of Higher Education Workforce 1997–2007*. Washington, D.C.: American Federation of Teachers, 2009. Retrieved December 8, 2011, from www.aftface.org/storage/face/documents/ameracad_report_97-07for_web.pdf.

Association of American Universities. *Non-Tenure-Track Faculty Report*. Washington, D.C.: Association of American Universities, 2001. Retrieved December 8, 2011, from www.aau.edu/WorkArea/DownloadAsset.aspx?id=466.

Baldwin, R. G., and Chronister, J. L. *Teaching Without Tenure*. Baltimore, Md.: Johns Hopkins University Press, 2001.

Berry, J. *Reclaiming the Ivory Tower: Organizing Adjuncts to Change Higher Education*. New York: Monthly Review Press, 2005.

Bettinger, E., and Long, B. T. *Do College Instructors Matter? The Effects of Adjuncts and Graduate Assistants on Students' Interests and Success*. NBER Working Paper No. 10370. Cambridge, Mass.: National Bureau of Economic Research, 2004.

Carrell, S. E., and West, J. E. "Does Professor Quality Matter? Evidence from Random Assignment of Students to Professors." *Journal of Political Economy*, 2010, *118*, 409–432.

Coalition on the Academic Workforce (CAW). *About the Coalition on the Academic Workforce*. n.d. Retrieved November 4, 2011, from www.academicworkforce.org/.

Cross, J. G., and Goldenberg, E. N. *Off-Track Profs: Non-Tenured Teachers in Higher Education*. Cambridge, Mass.: MIT Press, 2009.

Eagan, M. K., and Jaeger, A. J. "Effects of Exposure to Part-Time Faculty on Community College Transfer." *Research in Higher Education*, 2009, *50*, 168–188.

Ehrenberg, R. G., and Zhang, L. "Do Tenured and Tenure-Track Faculty Matter?" *Journal of Human Resources*, 2005, *45*(3), 647–659.

Gappa, J. M., and Leslie, D. W. *The Invisible Faculty: Improving the Status of Part Timers in Higher Education*. San Francisco: Jossey-Bass, 1993.

Harper, E. P., Baldwin, R. G., Gansneder, B. G., and Chronister, J. L. "Full-Time Women Faculty Off the Tenure Track: Profile and Practice." *Review of Higher Education*, 2001, *24*(3), 237–257.

Hollenshead and others. *Making the Best of Both Worlds: Findings from a National Institution-Level Survey on Non-Tenure-Track Faculty*. Ann Arbor, MI: Center for the Education of Women, 2007.

Jaeger, A., and Eagan, M. K. "Unintended Consequences: Examining the Effect of Part-Time Faculty Members on Associate's Degree Completion." *Community College Review*, 2009, *36*, 167–194.

Kezar, A. *Embracing Non-Tenure-Track Faculty: Changing Campuses for the New Faculty Majority*. New York: Routledge, 2012.

Kezar, A., and Sam, C. *Non-Tenure-Track Faculty in Higher Education*. San Francisco: Jossey-Bass, 2010a.

Kezar, A., and Sam, C. *Understanding the New Majority of Non-Tenure-Track Faculty in Higher Education.* San Francisco: Jossey-Bass, 2010b.

Kezar, A., and Sam, C. "Institutionalizing New Policies and Practices for Non-Tenure Track Faculty: Understanding the Change Process." In A. Kezar (ed.), *Embracing Non-Tenure-Track Faculty: Changing Campuses for the New Faculty Majority.* New York: Routledge, 2012.

National Education Association (NEA). *Higher Education Policy Statement on Part-Time, Temporary, and NTT Appointments.* Washington, D.C.: National Education Association, 2002.

National Education Association (NEA). *National Education Association and the Contingent Academic Workers: NB1 2004–60 Action Plan.* Washington, D.C.: National Education Association, 2004. Retrieved December 8, 2011, from www.nea.org/assets/docs/HE/neacontingentplan.pdf.

National Education Association (NEA). *Part-Time Faculty: A Look at Data and Issues.* Washington, D.C.: National Education Association, 2007. Retrieved December 8, 2011, from www.nea.org/assets/docs/HE/vol11no3.pdf.

New Faculty Majority (NFM). *New Faculty Majority: Our Mission.* n.d. Retrieved November 4, 2011, from www.newfacultymajority.info/national/.

Schuster, J. H., and Finkelstein, M. J. *American Faculty: The Restructuring of Academic Work and Careers.* Baltimore, Md.: Johns Hopkins University Press, 2006.

Shavers, F. L. "Academic Ranks and Titles of Full-Time Non-Tenure-Track Faculty." In S. Slaughter and G. Rhoades (eds.), *Academic Capitalism and the New Economy: Markets, State, and Higher Education.* Baltimore, Md.: Johns Hopkins University Press, 2000.

ADRIANNA KEZAR is associate professor for higher education at the University of Southern California.

DANIEL MAXEY is a doctoral student in urban education policy at the University of Southern California.

4

A better understanding of the professional life of women faculty is gained by comparing the work experiences of two subgroups: those working in disciplines considered "traditional" for women and those working in "nontraditional" disciplines.

The Similarities and Differences in the Work Experience of Women Faculty in Traditional and Nontraditional Disciplines

Yonghong Jade Xu

A myriad of studies have examined gender gaps in higher education faculties and documented gender-based inequity in salary, turnover, and other aspects of academic worklife (see, for example, August and Waltman, 2004; Gander, 1999; Hagedorn, 1996; Perna, 2001, 2005; Persell, 1983; Smart, 1991; Stack, 2004; Toutkoushian and Conely, 2005; Umbach, 2007; Xu, 2008). In recent years, increasing research attention has been given to the extremely low presence of women faculty in nontraditional disciplines including science, technology, engineering, and mathematics (see, for example, Fox and Mohapatra, 2007; Nelson and Rogers, 2005). A review of literature suggests that many disadvantages experienced by women faculty, such as earning lower salaries and working in lower ranks and nontenured positions, seem to be common across disciplines (see, for example, Bentley and Adamson, 2003; Perna, 2001; Rosser, 2003). One question raised by this observation is whether there are differences in the work experience of women faculty in traditional and nontraditional disciplines. The answer to this question may help to shed light on the strategic institutional interventions to increase the representation of women and decrease gender inequity in colleges and universities.

In this chapter, I explored and compared the work experiences of women faculty in fields of different gender compositions with data from three National Study of Postsecondary Faculty (NSOPF: 1993, 1999, and 2004) surveys. By examining the influence of a wide range of factors, this

NEW DIRECTIONS FOR INSTITUTIONAL RESEARCH, no. 155, Fall 2012 © Wiley Periodicals, Inc.
Published online in Wiley Online Library (wileyonlinelibrary.com) • DOI: 10.1002/ir.20022

study provides a comprehensive picture of the work experience of women faculty in nontraditional disciplines in comparison to their counterparts in traditional fields. It also traces the changes that have taken place for women and their underrepresentation in certain disciplines from a long-term perspective.

Gender Inequity Documented in the Literature

Gender Differences in Salary and Promotion. During the past few decades, numerous studies have been conducted to examine gender inequity in postsecondary faculty from various perspectives. The most inquired subject is gender-based salary disparity (see, for example, Bellas, 1997; Hagedorn, 1998; Perna, 2001; Smart, 1991; Toutkoushian, 1998; Toutkoushian and Conely, 2005; Umbach, 2007). Almost always, studies of salary inequity, controlled for the effects of human capital (for example, education, training, and job experience) and faculty productivity measures (Bentley and Adamson, 2003), and their findings have consistently supported the overall salary disadvantage of women faculty. When taking into consideration academic disciplines, some studies found that the average salary has a negative relationship with the percentage of women in the areas (Bellas, 1997; Smart, 1991). In one study, the author concluded that "faculty in disciplines with higher proportions of women suffer a financial penalty relative to those in disciplines where women are scarce" (Bellas, 1997, p. 315).

In the higher education setting, tenure and academic rank are proxy indicators of human capital accumulation, and they are often used as control variables in salary studies (Perna, 2003; see also Settles, Cortina, Malley, and Stewart, 2006). However, empirical evidence suggests gender inequity in tenure and promotion; women faculty, in general, are less likely to achieve tenure and to be promoted to higher ranks (Perna, 2001; Smart, 1991). The same statements hold true for women scientists in nontraditional disciplines (Bentley and Adamson, 2003; Pell, 1996). The unexplained gender gap in rank attainment remains even after measures of faculty research productivity, career age, and family-related factors are taken into consideration.

Gender Difference in Productivity. Performance and productivity of university faculty are vital factors in salary and promotion, which is part of the reason why they have been topics of debates and discussions (see, for example, Allen, 2009; Boyer, 1990; Fairweather, 1997, 2005; Gander, 1999; Hagedorn, 2001; Park, 1996; Persell, 1983). What is challenging for studies in this area is the multidimensionality of faculty responsibilities and the complexity in defining and measuring faculty productivity. University faculty members are expected to perform in teaching, research, and academic and community services. However, for faculty in all disciplines in four-year institutions, research and scholarly productivity dominate the equation for reward and promotion (Fairweather, 2005; Frehill, Javurek-Humig, and Jeser-Cannavale, 2006; Park, 1996; Persell, 1983). As such, the phrase "productivity puzzle" is coined to indicate, in the population of university faculty, the general trend that women *publish* less than men (Gander, 1999; Hagedorn, 2001; Park, 1996; Persell, 1983; Stack, 2004; Xie and Shauman, 2003). Even though women faculty are found to have disproportionately heavier teaching loads, not only in the classroom but also in terms of time spent on advising and preparing for classes (Park, 1996), it is apparent that it is not enough to save women from any disadvantages associated with having "low" research productivity. More time committed to service activities is another consistent conclusion in studies of women faculty in comparison to their male counterparts (Park, 1996; Rosser, 2003).

With that said, it seems more disadvantageous for women faculty in nontraditional disciplines in which an even stronger emphasis on research productivity is perceived (Barbezat, 1992). Similar to the "productivity puzzle" in general, women scientists are found to have fewer publications and less grant support than their male colleagues (Bentley and Adamson, 2003; Pell, 1996; Sonnert and Holton, 1995). Scholarly discussions of potential causes include the usual suspects such as heavier teaching and services responsibilities and family factors. Nonetheless, a unique dimension to scientific research activities is the importance of collaboration with others (Fox and Mohapatra, 2007). In other words, the social and organizational features of scientific research activities render the success of faculty members dependent on the availability of research support in terms of human and materials resources. As Lewis (2003) stated, "Science career attainment is a social process" (p. 371). For women faculty in nontraditional fields, the dilemma is that men control power and access to resources, and women remain in marginalized positions with limited power to become resourceful in research supports (Frehill, Javurek-Humig, and Jeser-Cannavale, 2005).

Family Responsibility and Child Rearing. Studies have also shown the complex tension found in balancing work and family roles for women faculty (Perna, 2001). A survey study by Rosser (2003) confirmed that across disciplines, most women faculty self-reported that balancing work and family responsibilities was one of the most significant challenges as they plan their career. The general pattern is that women assume greater parental and marital responsibilities (Bellas and Toutkoushian, 1999; Perna, 2001; Stack, 2004). Family responsibility and childbearing are suspected to distract women from their professional endeavor (National Research Council, 1991), even though findings have not been consistent in this regard (Frehill, Javurek-Humig, and Jeser-Cannavale, 2006; Pell, 1996). For instance, married faculty have been found to have higher productivity than those who are single (Bellas and Toutkoushian, 1999; Sax, Hagedorn, Arredondo, and Dicrisi, 2002). However, research also shows that family responsibilities and childbearing may negatively affect faculty's careers in terms of mobility and professional advancement (Marshall and Jones, 1990; Perna, 2001).

In a qualitative study of the academic career paths of scientists from their postdoctoral and beyond, Sonnert and Holton (1995) suggested that personal and family issues had a much more practical and stronger impact on the career of women scientists than on those of men. However, some researchers (see, for example, Zuckerman, 1991) argued that, having committed to an academic career in nontraditional disciplines, women scientists have already figured out a way to maintain their scholarly productivity while taking care of family responsibilities. It is the gender-biased *notion* that women are unable to meet the work demands and family commitments simultaneously that plays a role in the inequality that they experience in hiring and promotion.

Perceived Work Environment and Job Satisfaction. Marginalization and inequity experienced by women faculty at work have resulted in some severe consequences, including low job satisfaction and high attrition rate (August and Waltman, 2004). In fact, job satisfaction is a complex and convoluted construct that has been empirically linked with many psychological and behavioral consequences, including workplace morale, turnover rate, productivity, and work quality (August and Waltman, 2004; Hagedorn, 2000; Johnsrud and Rosser, 2002; Rosser, 2004; Smart, 1990). The emphasis is that the objective work conditions affect personal behavioral outcomes through the intermediation of sociopsychological variables such as perceived fairness and satisfaction (Daly and Dee, 2006; Rosser, 2004; Smart, 1990; Seifert and Umbach, 2008). Therefore, it is necessary to examine faculty members' subjective evaluation, including satisfaction with job and work environment, in order to understand how personal perceptions of support, leadership, and equity issues affect women faculty's attitude, effectiveness, and productivity.

For women in nontraditional disciplines, the social and organizational bases for research activities (Fox and Mohapatra, 2007) make the "chilly climate" more inevitable. As suggested by a "deficit model" (Settles, Cortina, Malley, and Stewart, 2006; Sonnert and Holton, 1996), in order to succeed in a male-dominated academic culture, women have to overcome formal and informal cultural or organizational mechanisms that materialize their minority status in isolation and marginalization, fewer opportunities, limited support, and inequity in accessing resources and leadership. Given the isolation and marginalization of underrepresented minority and the possible outcomes associated with job satisfaction, it would be interesting to investigate whether women faculty have lower job satisfaction in areas where they have minority status than those women who are the numeric majority at work.

Research Interests. Strong empirical evidence supports that women faculty members share negative experiences and encounter a "glass ceiling" regardless of their disciplines (see, for example, Hagedorn, 2001; Perna, 2005). As documented in the literature, a wide spectrum of factors has been identified in relation to gender inequity in academia, including demographic and professional factors, work productivity, reward and promotion, and subjective evaluation of the work environment.

Extant research—whether studying women faculty in general or studying women in male-dominated areas—keeps the contrast and comparison between women and their male counterparts. Rarely is there any interest in understanding how women's experiences differ across disciplines. Given the argument about women's inability to compel changes from within when their level of presence is lower than a "critical mass" (at least 15 percent) in a unit (Kanter, 1977; see also Kulis, Sicotte, and Collins, 2002; Nelson and Rogers, 2005), it is suspected that women faculty might have distinct work environments and professional experience in areas where they no longer have minority status. Thus, in this study, I examine the work experiences of women faculty in areas of different gender compositions and, through this unique perspective, uncover potential causes of women's low presence in nontraditional disciplines.

Method

This study used NSOPF 1993, 1999, and 2004 data from a survey program sponsored by the National Center of Educational Statistics (NCES) to gather information about postsecondary faculty members with regard to the various aspects of their professional lives and demographic backgrounds. Each of the three implementations started with a nationally representative sample of postsecondary faculty selected from two-year and four-year public and nonprofit private institutions with stratified sampling procedures. The numbers of faculty surveyed and the weighted response rates for the three surveys are approximately 31,400 and 84 percent in 1993, 28,600 and 83 percent in 1999, and 35,000 and 76 percent in 2004.

In this study, the sample was limited to full-time women faculty members with primary responsibility in either teaching or research at Research and Doctoral universities. The selection of this subgroup of faculty is based on the considerations that (1) research and doctoral universities share similar academic culture and reward structure that require faculty performance in research, teaching, and service (Rosser, 2004); and (2) research-oriented universities have the strongest gender disparity in their science and engineering programs (Bentley and Adamson, 2003; Nelson and Rogers, 2005). Given the stratifications in sampling, the data were weighted in both descriptive and inferential analysis, and the weighted sample sizes are 901, 1,046, and 1,578 from the NSOPF 1993, 1999, and 2004 data, respectively. Additional descriptive information is available in Table 4.1.

Table 4.1. Differences in the Work Experience of Women Faculty in 1993, 1999, and 2004

		Group 1	Group 2	Group 3	Group 4
		Percentage of Women Faculty			
		1–24%	25–49%	50–74%	75–100%
Count (weighted)	1993	235	504	72	92
	1999	176	602	212	92
	2004	451	802	260	132
Total credit hours[a]	1993	5.30	6.27	7.49	7.94
Undergraduate classroom	1999	6.44	3.91	11.78	6.64
credit hours	2004	3.61	4.76	2.95	4.31
Percentage of time spent on	1993	37.15	28.82	17.70	14.78
research	1999	31.58	30.33	15.63	13.17
	2004	38.14	28.52	30.82	19.43
Career total refereed	1993	13.34	10.00	7.73	3.40
publications	1999	16.18	16.72	10.78	13.17
	2004	18.45	12.87	15.92	7.55
Age	1993	42.64	44.45	45.49	47.97
	1999	43.20	46.43	47.80	51.42
	2004	45.21	46.79	48.69	50.50
Salary[b]	1993	44092.63	42292.26	39181.10	38320.60
	1999	52100.95	58389.19	43958.40	48852.34
	2004	65647.65	61467.83	61973.40	55207.92
Satisfaction with research	1993	5.84	5.22	4.57	5.55
support[c]	1999	10.34	9.74	10.35	9.27
	2004				

[a] The significant measure of teaching activity is total classroom credit hours in the 1993 model and changed to undergraduate classroom credit hours in 1999 and 2004 models.
[b] Salary of 1993 was included for comparison purpose only.
[c] Satisfaction with research support is not available in NSOPF 2004.

Defining "Nontraditional" Disciplines. In the literature, there are a few classification methods of academic disciplines that might help to define "nontraditional fields." For instance, Biglan's (1973) model groups all disciplines into eight clusters according to three dimensional measures: *Hard* vs. *Soft*, *Pure* vs. *Applied*, and *Life* vs. *Nonlife* (Umbach, 2007; Xu, 2008). Disciplines in the "Hard" cluster are usually considered as "nontraditional" to women. The acronym *STEM* has gained great popularity as it stands for science, technology, engineering, and mathematics, areas with low participation from women in general. However, both approaches may heighten or obscure gender contrasts (Kulis, Sicotte, and Collins, 2002) and overlook the considerable variations of women's participation among fields. For example, biology has a high concentration of women even though it is classified as hard science (Bentley and Adamson, 2003; Frehill, Javurek-Humig, and Jeser-Cannavale, 2006; Rosser, 2003). Taking into consideration the research focus on women scientists and the "critical mass" argument (Kanter, 1977; see also

Kulis, Sicotte, and Collins, 2002; Nelson and Rogers, 2005), I decided to classify the approximately 140 academic programs in NSOPF into four groups based on the percentage of women in the program: (1) extremely low presence (0 percent to 24 percent), (2) moderately low presence (25 percent to 49 percent), (3) moderately high presence (50 percent to 74 percent), and (4) high presence (75 percent to 100 percent). Programs in the four groups include different *gender compositions*, and those in the "extremely low presence" group are defined as *nontraditional fields* for women.

Method of Analysis. The NSOPF data were collected at three different time points and they were not from the same sample, but *three random samples taken from the population over time*. The different samples render longitudinal analysis inappropriate. Therefore, in order to take advantage of three cross-sections of a national faculty, this study uses Bayesian Network (BN), one type of nonparametric application of Bayesian probability (Williamson and Corfield, 2001), to model the work environment of women faculty from a long-term perspective.

Bayesian probability is a set of probability rules originated from Bayes' Theorem. Bayesian probability enables a process of incorporating new information into current knowledge for a more accurate classification and/or prediction about unknown events through probability rules (that is, product rule, sum rule, and Bayes' rule). For example, the NSOPF 2004 sample shows that approximately 37 percent of full-time faculty are tenured, so 0.37 would be the likelihood of being correct when classifying a randomly selected faculty member as tenured without any other knowledge about the individual. That is, the *prior* probability or $p(E) = 0.37$, where E is the event of "having tenure." To increase the classification accuracy, additional information from the data can be useful. For instance, 81 percent of associate professors are tenured. The new information (academic rank of an individual) contributes to a more accurate classification: $p(E \mid C) = 0.81$, where C is the condition of "being an associate professor." Here, $p(E \mid C)$ is called conditional probability, the probability of E given C is true; and $p(E \mid C) = 0.81$ is the posterior probability in Bayesian terminology.

In mathematical language, the posterior **probability** is calculated by Bayes' rule:

$$p(E \mid C) = \frac{p(C \mid E)p(E)}{p(C)}$$

In more extended versions, Bayes' rule can chain more useful information together (for example, productivity, salary) in the format of joint probabilities (Western, 1999). The classification outcome (for example, group defined by percentage of females) is expressed as a probability—the posterior probability. BN, the analytical procedure used in this study, is a chain of Bayesian probabilities expressed in a tree-like network (Williamson and Corfield, 2001).

NEW DIRECTIONS FOR INSTITUTIONAL RESEARCH • DOI: 10.1002/ir

As a classification model, BN has several advantages (Friedman, Geiger, and Goldszmidt, 1997). First, BN is a flexible technique for handling different types of variables. This modeling approach works best with nominal or ordinal variables, whereas interval and ratio variables need to be binned into a number of discrete intervals. The binning of continuous variables frees BN models from parametric requirements such as linearity and normality, which makes this approach robust against outliers and other noisy data structures (Williamson and Corfield, 2001). Second, unlike linear statistical models that consider predictor variables independently or with a limited number of interaction effects, BN models can simultaneously test a relatively large number of variables, examine all possible variable correlations, and depict the important connections in the final models (Williamson and Corfield, 2001). Finally, a BN model can be expressed visually as a network of significantly related variables (Heckerman, 1997; Press, 2004). The connections between variables are directional and indicate causal/relevance relationships. Although it is unwise to infer causality using survey data, Bayesian models are sensitive to the directions of variable relationships. Similar to structural equation modeling (SEM), inferences about causality may be possible with theoretical support.

Variables. Based on the review of literature, five clusters of variables are included in the analysis. The first cluster includes three demographic variables—age, marital status, and number of dependents of a faculty member. Measures of academic seniority, including tenure status, academic rank, highest degree type, and years in current position, are considered as human capital indicators in the second cluster. A number of variables related to work productivity are in the third cluster, including an individual's principal activity (that is, research or teaching), number of undergraduate credit hours, number of graduate credit hours, number of total classroom credit hours, percentage of time for research, career total refereed publications, Principal Investigator (PI)/Co-PI status, and time spent on administrative committees. *Salary* is in the fourth cluster to reflect institutional reward for an individual's work performance. The final group of variables is *personal perceptions of the work environment* measured as self-reported rating of research support, faculty leadership, gender equity, and job satisfaction.

Analytical Procedures. The analysis is carried out in three consecutive steps:

1. Every respondent in the 1993, 1999, and 2004 data is assigned a group membership (1 = extremely low presence, 2 = moderately low presence, 3 = moderately high presence, and 4 = high presence) based on the percentage of women in the program to which they belonged.
2. With the group membership defined in step 1 being the output variable, a baseline BN model is built with women faculty members in

the 1993 data set. The modeling process begins with all predictor variables included, and the final model retains only those that are the manifestation of major differences in the work experience of women faculty in programs of different gender compositions.

3. The generalizability of the baseline model is tested with 1999 and 2004 data. The model classification accuracy with the recent data should be close to that of the 1993 data if the model is generalizable over time. Classification accuracy is defined as the percentage of observations being classified into the right output group. If the baseline models have low classification accuracy with the recent data, the analyses in Step 2 are to be repeated with the 1999 and 2004 data. The structures of the models built on data from different years are compared to benchmarks and monitored over time.

Results

The final baseline BN model is composed of six predictor variables and classifies 76.5 percent of the women faculty members into the correct group of gender composition (see Figure 4.1). All six predictor variables are a direct display of differences among women in the four groups of disciplines of different gender compositions: age, career total refereed publications, percentage of time spent on research, satisfaction with research support, total classroom credit hours, and highest degree type. Three of the six variables are research related. As shown in Table 4.1, the general trend is that, with increased women's presence in the fields, the average teaching load for women increased, whereas time spent on research and the number of refereed publications decreased. Further analysis is conducted and Scheffe's tests support that women in nontraditional fields spent significantly more time

Figure 4.1. Baseline BN Model of Women in Disciplines of Different Gender Compositions (NSOPF:93)

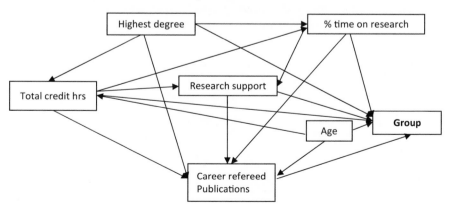

($p < 0.001$) on research, had more refereed publications ($p < 0.001$), and rated research support more positively ($p = 0.016$) than their counterparts in other fields. In contrast, the teaching load of women faculty in nontraditional fields was significantly lower than those in other fields ($p < 0.001$). Clearly, this baseline model depicts the major difference in work experiences of women faculty in traditional and nontraditional disciplines as the different assignments of research and teaching activities.

When tested with the 1999 data, the classification accuracy of the baseline model is reduced to 41.2 percent, an indication that changes have taken place from 1993 to 1999. The baseline model cannot be validated with the 2004 data because one of the predictor variables, satisfaction with research support, is unavailable in this survey. Separate BN models are constructed from the 1999 and 2004 data. The 1999 model (Figure 4.2) has 78.6 percent classification accuracy and the 2004 model (Figure 4.3) 75.3 percent. The 1999 and 2004 models are very similar; both have age, career total refereed publications, percentage of time spent on research, undergraduate credit hours, salary, and highest degree type. One of the predictor variables in the 1999 model, satisfaction with research support, was removed from the 2004 implementation of the NSOPF survey and is not in the 2004 BN model.

The 1993, 1999, and 2004 models share most of the predictor variables. Comparisons of the models show that interesting changes took place over time. First, one major difference from the baseline model to the others is that salary difference in 1993 was not strong enough to set women faculty apart into the four groups. Second, as shown in Table 4.1, from 1993 to 1999, women faculty in group 2 experienced strong changes, shown as lower teaching assignment, increased time for research (30.3 in 1999 versus 28.8 in 1993), higher number of refereed publications (16.7 in 1999 versus 10.0 in 1993), dramatic increase in salary ($58,389 in 1999 versus $42,292 in 1993), and heightened satisfaction with

Figure 4.2. BN Model of Women Faculty in Disciplines of Different Gender Compositions (NSOPF:99)

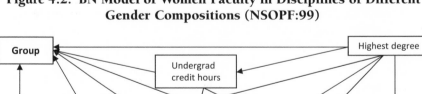

Figure 4.3. BN Model of Women Faculty in Disciplines of Different Gender Compositions (NSOPF:04)

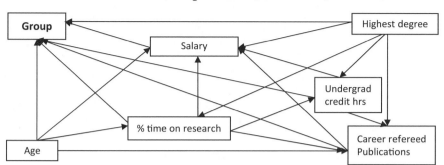

research support (9.74 in 1999 versus 5.22 in 1993). However, for those in nontraditional disciplines with extremely low women's presence (group 1), unfavorable changes were observed and the teaching load, measured as undergraduate classroom credit hours, was increased to 6.44, even higher than the total credit hours of the same group (5.30) in 1993. As a result, their time spent on research decreased from 37.1 percent to 31.6 percent. As time went on from 1999 to 2004, the tide made another turn. Women in group 1 had significantly increased salary ($65,648 in 2004 versus $52,101 in 1999), reduced undergraduate teaching responsibility (3.61 in 2004 versus 6.44 in 1999), more time for research (38.1 percent in 2004 versus 31.6 percent in 1999), and higher publication records (18.5 in 2004 versus 16.2 in 1999). However, the advantages of women in group 2 in 1999 disappeared; as a group they had the highest undergraduate classroom credit hours (4.76 in 2004), reduced time on research, decreased number of refereed publications, and smallest salary increase (only about $3,087) in comparison to women in other groups.

Several general trends stayed consistent over the decade (see Table 4.1). First, women in male-dominated disciplines spent more time on research, had more publications, and had lighter teaching assignments in comparison to their counterparts in areas with higher women presence. Second, the average salary for women shows a negative relationship with the percentage of women faculty in a discipline. Finally, across all disciplines, research as part of the faculty responsibility becomes more emphasized and, as such, faculty spent more time on research activities and published more. Those who reported higher satisfaction with research support also had more refereed publications.

Discussion

Differences Across Discipline Groups. The major differences in the work experience of women faculty in disciplines of various gender compositions are shown in their teaching assignments, time committed to research activities, career total refereed publications, and satisfaction with research support. Overall, women in nontraditional fields spend more time on research and have more publications—a clear sign that there is a stronger discipline commitment to research and scholarly activities. However, some trends of change are not very encouraging. First, for women faculty in group 1, where their presence is lower than 25 percent, teaching load was increased and time spent on research decreased from 1993 to 1999. Even though they managed to keep up their research productivity, the magnitude of increased productivity was behind their counterparts in other disciplines. Along with the ever-increasing emphasis on research activities, those changes in teaching and research time may have translated into elevated job stress and attrition rates.

Second, women faculty in disciplines in group 2 remain the numeric minority with a lower than 50 percent presence (25 percent to 49 percent). The speculation based on the findings is that some effort was made after 1993 to increase women's presence in those disciplines. As part of the results, women faculty had reduced teaching responsibilities, were able to increase their research productivity with more time allocated to research, and had a significant salary hike in comparison to their counterparts in other groups. However, the improvements did not last long. From 1999 to 2004, women in the same group not only lost their salary advantages but also reported a lower number of publications, as well as increased teaching load and reduced time for research. It is possible that some program areas in group 2, after substantive efforts were made to attract and retain more women faculty, increased women's presence from lower than 50 percent in 1999 to higher than 50 percent and moved into groups 3 and 4 in 2004 data.

The fact that positive changes in group 2 from 1993 to 1999 have been reversed in the following years requires a look at the "critical mass" argument from a different angle. According to the "critical mass" argument, with a minority presence of 15 percent or less in a unit, female faculty do not have sufficient power to impact the organizational culture and policy from within (Kanter, 1977; Kulis, Sicotte, and Collins, 2002; Nelson and Rogers, 2005). Albeit the percentages of women faculty exceeded the critical mass in disciplines in group 2, they still were unable to secure a more gender-friendly workplace. In contrast, women in group 1 were better off from 1999 to 2004. The indication is that a higher percentage of women, in and of itself, would not simply offset cultural and environmental factors that negatively affect women in the academic settings. Institutional attention and public pressure, stimulated by studies like this one, are necessary to press for policy changes and to promote an academic culture that provides equal opportunity for women scientists.

Further comparison across models suggests that research has increased importance in faculty work regardless of disciplines. Women faculty spent more time on research activities and were provided better research supports, and those who were more satisfied with research support had more refereed publications. Thus, it is important to provide sufficient resources and support to women faculty in order to increase their research productivity and eliminate "productivity puzzles" in the long run.

Findings of the study also suggest that the salary of women faculty is significantly different across disciplines, with a general trend showing the average salary having a negative relationship with the percentage of women in the areas, confirming the conclusions of previous research (see, for example, Bellas, 1997; Smart, 1991). It should not be taken as a comfort that women in the nontraditional disciplines earned the highest salary among the four groups; market value determines the average salary level for academic disciplines (Youn, 1992), and an analysis of the same data has revealed women still earn lower salary in comparison to their male colleagues (Xu, 2010).

Similarities Among Discipline Groups. Across disciplines, women faculty do not have strong differences in terms of their marital status and number of dependents. This trend can be interpreted from two aspects. On the one hand, women faculty experience similar challenges in balancing work and family responsibilities, regardless of their academic disciplines. On the other hand, the notion that women have to give up family life and completely commit to work in order to be a successful scientist/scholar in nontraditional disciplines is misleading and detrimental. It is possible that, as Sonnert and Holton (1996) argued, broad variables such as marital status and number of dependents are not sufficient enough to capture the complex and idiosyncratic interactions between family responsibility and a science career. Nonetheless, many women faculty have demonstrated their ability to balance work and family by being successful scholars and responsible mothers/wives simultaneously.

None of the four human capital variables (that is, tenure status, academic rank, highest degree type, and years in current position) show significant differences for women faculty in the programs of different gender compositions. In other words, within the four groups, the distributions of women faculty across academic ranks and across tenure groups are very similar. Analysis of the same data (Xu, 2010) found that women concentrated in low ranks and nontenured positions. Thus, the indication here is that across disciplines women faculty experience the similar inequity: they are less likely to achieve tenure and to be promoted to higher ranks (Perna, 2001; Smart, 1991).

Implications for Institutional Researchers and Administrators. This study does not produce any findings to challenge the common knowledge of the inequity experienced by women faculty; rather, it highlights the emphasis on scholarly activity and research productivity in nontraditional disciplines. Women faculty in nontraditional disciplines spend more time on research and have more publications in refereed media than their counterparts in areas of higher presence of women. However, fluctuation of teaching and research productivities by women in nontraditional fields through the year, as shown in the analysis, suggests that institutional researchers may need to constantly provide evidence to convince administrators that fair assignment of teaching, research, and services responsibilities is critical in order to increase the number of women scientists in nontraditional disciplines.

Additionally, given the role played by institutional research in planning and policymaking, IR officers can help women faculty by highlighting the importance of research supports (for example, resources and collaboration opportunities) to their career success. The underrepresentation of women in nontraditional disciplines should be confronted by a joint effort of campus administers, researchers, and faculty members, given that "it can be argued that science constitutes a critical and strategic test of gender equity issues in academia because debates about whether gender differences in academic careers are due principally to labor supply, institutional forces, or individual differences in scholarly merit are no more sharply drawn than in science" (Kulis, Sicotte, and Collins, 2002, p. 681).

Last but not least, IR officers need to work with other campus agencies to ensure consistent and effective enforcement of gender equity interventions and policies. The reverse of the positive changes that took place from 1993 to 1999 in later years for women faculty in group 2 is a warning sign against the notion that achieving equity is simply a matter of a yearly report on and quick fix of faculty salary. Long-term planning is required because, in essence, equity is a cultural transformation that takes time and collective efforts. Particularly, for women in male-dominated disciplines, equity means radical changes to an academic culture that isolates women and disconnects them from power and resource centers (Ibarra, 1993; Mehra, Kilduff, and Brass, 1998). As Barber (1995) argued, in order to provide a healthy and supportive environment to women scientists, institutional interventions should focus on broadening and diversifying the cultural norm of male-dominated disciplines. In other words, through their data collection and research activities, institutional researchers ought to help the campus community understand that it is the embrace of gender equity and gender difference by academic and organizational culture that will bring forward long-lasting changes and dissolve inequity from the roots.

Acknowledgment

This research was supported by a grant from the American Educational Research Association which received funds for its "AERA Grants Program" from the National Science Foundation and the National Center for Education Statistics of the Institute of Education Science (U.S. Department of Education) under NSF Grant #REC-0634035. Opinions reflect those of the author and do not necessarily reflect those of the granting agencies.

References

Allen, H. L. "Faculty Workload and Productivity: The Next Generation's Plight—and Opportunity." *The NEA 2009 Almanac of Higher Education*, 2009. Retrieved April 1, 2010, from www.nea.org/home/32967.htm.

August, L., and Waltman, J. "Culture, Climate, and Contribution: Career Satisfaction Among Female Faculty." *Research in Higher Education*, 2004, *45*(2), 177–192.

Barbezat, D. A. "The Market for New Ph.D. Economists." *Journal of Economic Education*, 1992, Summer, 262–275.

Barber, L. A. "U. S. Women in Science and Engineering, 1960–1990: Progress Toward Equity?" *Journal of Higher Education*, 1995, *66*(2), 213–234.

Bellas, M. L. "Disciplinary Differences in Faculty Salaries: Does Gender Play a Role?" *Journal of Higher Education*, 1997, *68*(3), 299–321.

Bellas, M. L., and Toutkoushian, R. K. "Family Time Allocations and Research Productivity: Gender, Race, and Family Effects." *Review of Higher Education*, 1999, *22*(4), 367–390.

Bentley, J. T., and Adamson, R. *Gender Differences in the Careers of Academic Scientists and Engineers: A Literature Review.* Special Report (NSF 00-327). Arlington, VA: NSF, 2003.

Biglan, A. "The Characteristics of Subject Matter in Different Academic Areas." *Journal of Applied Psychology*, 1973, *57*(3), 195–203.

Boyer, E. L. *Scholarship Reconsidered: Priorities of the Professoriate.* Princeton, N.J.: Carnegie Foundation for the Advancement of Teaching, 1990.

Daly, C., and Dee, J. R. "Greener Pastures: Faculty Turnover Intent in Urban Public Universities." *Journal of Higher Education*, 2006, *77*(5), 776–803.

Fairweather, J. S. "The Value of Teaching, Research, and Service." In H. Wechsler (ed.), *The NEA 1997 Almanac of Higher Education.* Washington, D.C.: National Education Association, 1997.

Fairweather, J. S. "Beyond the Rhetoric: Trends in the Relative Value of Teaching and Research in Faculty Salaries." *Journal of Higher Education*, 2005, *76*(4), 401–422.

Fox, M. F., and Mohapatra, S. "Social-Organizational Characteristics of Work and Publication Productivity Among Academic Scientists in Doctoral-Granting Departments." *Journal of Higher Education*, 2007, *78*(5), 542–571.

Frehill, L., Javurek-Humig, A., and Jeser-Cannavale, C. "Women in Engineering: A Review of the 2005 Literature." *Magazine of the Society of Women Engineering*, 2006, *52*(3), 34–63.

Friedman, N., Geiger, D., and Goldszmidt, M. "Bayesian Network Classifiers." *Machine Learning*, 1997, *29*(2–3), 131–163.

Gander, J. P. "Faculty Gender Effects on Academic Research and Teaching." *Research in Higher Education*, 1999, *40*(2), 171–184.

Hagedorn, L. S. "Wage Equity and Female Job Satisfaction: The Role of Wage Differentials in a Job Satisfaction Causal Model." *Research in Higher Education*, 1996, *37*(5), 569–598.

Hagedorn, L. S. "Implications to Postsecondary Faculty of Alternative Calculation Methods of Gender-Based Wage Differentials." *Research in Higher Education*, 1998, *39*(2), 143–162.

Hagedorn, L. S. "Conceptualizing Faculty Job Satisfaction: Components, Theories, and Outcomes." In L. S. Hagedorn (ed.), *What Contributes to Job Satisfaction Among Faculty and Staff.* San Francisco: Jossey-Bass, 2000.

Hagedorn, L. S. *Gender Differences in Faculty Productivity, Satisfaction, and Salary: What Really Separates Us?* 2001. Retrieved September 24, 2006, from http://eric.ed.gov/. (ED 464 548).

Heckerman, D. "Bayesian Networks for Data Mining." *Data Mining and Knowledge Discovery*, 1997, *1*, 79–119.

Ibarra, H. "Personal Networks of Women and Minorities in Management: A Conceptual Framework." *Academy of Management Review*, 1993, *18*(1), 56–87.

Johnsrud, L. K., and Rosser, V. J. "Faculty Members Morale and Their Intentions to Leave: A Multilevel Explanation." *Journal of Higher Education*, 2002, *71*(1), 34–59.

Kanter, R. M. *Men and Women of the Corporation.* New York: Basic Books, 1977.

Kulis, S., Sicotte, D., and Collins, S. "More Than a Pipeline Problem: Labor Supply Constraints and Gender Stratification across Academic Science Disciplines." *Research in Higher Education*, 2002, *43*(6), 657–690.

Lewis, B. F. "A Critique of the Literature on the Underrepresentation of African Americans in Science: Directions for Future Research." *Journal of Women and Minorities in Science and Engineering*, 2003, *9*, 361–373.

Marshall, M. R., and Jones, C. H. "Childbearing Sequence and the Career Development of Women Administrators in Higher Education." *Journal of College Student Development*, 1990, *31*, 531–537.

Mehra, A., Kilduff, M., and Brass, D. J. "At the Margins: A Distinctiveness Approach to the Social Identity and Social Networks of Underrepresented Groups." *Academy of Management Review*, 1998, *41*(4), 441–452.

National Research Council, Committee on Women in Science and Engineering. *Women in Science and Engineering: Increasing Their Numbers in the 1990s.* Washington, D.C.: National Academy Press, 1991.

Nelson, D., and Rogers, D. *A National Analysis of Diversity in Science and Engineering Faculties at Research Universities.* University of Oklahoma, Department of Chemistry, 2005. Retrieved March 06, 2006, from http://cheminfo.chem.ou.edu/~djn/diversity/briefings/Diversity%20Report%20Final.pdf.

Park, S. M. "Research, Teaching, and Service: Why Shouldn't Women's Work Count?" *Journal of Higher Education*, 1996, *67*(1), 46–84.

Pell, A. N. "Fixing the Leaky Pipeline: Women Scientists in Academia." *Journal of Animal Science*, 1996, *74*, 2843–2848.

Perna, L. W. "The Relationship Between Family Responsibility and Employment Status among College and University Faculty." *Journal of Higher Education*, 2001, *72*(5), 584–611.

Perna, L. W. "Studying Faculty Salary Equity: A Review of Theoretical and Methodological Approaches." In J. C. Smart (ed.), *Higher Education: Handbook of Theory and Research* (Vol. XVIII). Boston: Kluwer Academic Publishers, 2003.

Perna, L. W. "Sex Differences in Faculty Tenure and Promotion: The Contribution of Family Ties." *Research in Higher Education*, 2005, *46*(3), 277–306.

Persell, C. H. "Gender, Rewards, and Research in Education." *Psychology of Women Quarterly*, 1983, *8*(1), 33–47.

Press, J. "The Role of Bayesian and Frequentist Multivariate Modeling in Statistical Data Mining." In H. Bozdogan (ed.), *Statistical Data Mining and Knowledge Discovery.* Boca Raton, Fla.: CRC Press, 2004.

Rosser, S. V. "Attracting and Retaining Women in Science and Engineering." *Academe*, 2003, *89*(4), 24–28.

Rosser, V. J. "Faculty Members' Intentions to Leave: A National Study on Their Worklife and Satisfaction." *Research in Higher Education*, 2004, *45*(3), 285–309.

Sax, L. J., Hagedorn, L. S., Arredondo, M., and Dicrisi, F. A. III "Faculty Research Productivity: Exploring the Role of Gender and Family-Related Factors." *Research in Higher Education*, 2002, *43*(4), 423–446.

Seifert, T., and Umbach, P. (2008). "The Effects of Faculty Demographic Characteristics and Disciplinary Context on Dimensions of Job Satisfaction." *Research in Higher Education*, 49(4), 357–381.

Settles, I. H., Cortina, L. M., Malley, J., and Stewart, A. J. "The Climate for Women in Academic Science: The Good, the Bad, and the Changeable." *Psychology of Women Quarterly*, 2006, *30*, 47–58.

Smart. J. C. "A Causal Model of Faculty Turnover Intentions." *Research in Higher Education*, 1990, *31*(5), 405–424.

Smart, J. C. "Gender Equity in Academic Rank and Salary." *Review of Higher Education*, 1991, *14*(4), 511–525.

Sonnert, G., and Holton, G. "Who Succeeds in Science? The Gender Dimension." *American Scientists*, 1995, *84*(1), 63–71.

Sonnert, G., and Holton, G. *Career Patterns of Women and Men in the Sciences*. New Brunswick, N.J.: Rutgers University Press, 1996.

Stack, S. "Gender, Children and Research Productivity." *Research in Higher Education*, 2004, *45*(8), 891–920.

Toutkoushian, R. K. "A Summary of Two Studies on Pay Disparities by Race and Gender: Evidence From the 1998 and 1993 NCES Surveys." Paper presented at the Annual Meeting of the Association for Institutional Research, Minneapolis, Minn., May 1998.

Toutkoushian, R., K., and Conely, V. M. "Progress for Women in Academe, Yet Inequities Persist: Evidence from NSOPF:99." *Research in Higher Education*, 2005, *46*(1), 1–28.

Umbach, P. D. "Gender Equity in the Academic Labor Market: An Analysis of Academic Disciplines." *Research in Higher Education*, 2007, *48*(2), 169–192.

Western, B. "Bayesian Analysis for Sociologists: An Introduction." *Sociological Methods and Research*, 1999, *28*(1), 7–34.

Williamson, J., and Corfield, D. "Introduction: Bayesian Into the 21st Century." In D. Corfield and J. Williamson (eds.), *Foundations of Bayesianism*. Boston: Kluwer Academic Publishers, 2001.

Xie, Y., and Shauman, K. *Women in Science*. Cambridge, Mass.: Harvard University Press, 2003.

Xu, Y. "Gender Disparity in STEM Disciplines: A Study of Faculty Attrition and Turnover Intentions." *Research in Higher Education*, 2008, *49*(7), 607–624.

Xu, Y. "Understanding the Work Experience of Women Faculty in Nontraditional Fields: Bayesian Modeling of the 1993, 1999, and 2004 NSOPF Data." In S. A. Davies (ed.), *Gender Gap: Causes, Experiences and Effects*. New York: Nova Science Publishers, 2010.

Youn, Y.I.K. "Studies of Academic Markets and Careers: An Historical Review." In D. W. Breneman, and T. I. K. Youn (eds.), *Academic Labor Markets and Careers*. New York: Falmer Press, 1992.

Zuckerman, H. "The Careers of Men and Women Scientists: A Review of Current Research." In H. Zuckerman, J. R. Cole, and J. T. Bruer (eds.), *The Outer Circle: Women in the Scientific Community*. New York: W. W. Norton, 1991.

YONGHONG JADE XU is an associate professor of educational research at the University of Memphis.

In this chapter, a qualitative inquiry about the emotional management of minority faculty in a science department illustrates the value of qualitative methodology in conducting institutional research.

Emotional Management and Motivation: A Case Study of Underrepresented Faculty

Vicente M. Lechuga

The link between emotion and motivation has been well established in the psychology, management, and human resources literature (Bierema, 2001; Callahan and McCollum, 2002; Neumann, 2006). For instance, Jarvis (2006) suggests, "Emotions can have a considerable effect on the way we think, on motivation and on beliefs, attitudes and values" (p. 102). Similarly, Callahan and McCollum (2002) contend that, "the essence of motivation is emotion," further adding, "This stance is consistent with the research in the field of psychology, which posits that motivation is one of the primary functions of emotion" (p. 7). Erickson and Ritter (2001) noted the importance of investigating "specific emotions rather than treating 'emotion' as a monolithic concept" (p. 159) as has been discussed in much of the literature.

The influence of emotions in the workplace rarely has been examined within the context of higher education (Neumann, 2006; Smith and Witt, 1993). In their study of a subdimension of emotions, Smith and Witt (1993) explored the "stresses that arise from psychological and social processes that result from the personal interactions with others within the occupational environment" (p. 232), and found that black faculty members are subject to higher stress levels in teaching and research than their white counterparts. Neumann (2006) showed that scholarly work is emotional in content and put forth the notion of *passionate thought* as a framework for understanding faculty members' emotional work experiences, specifically during periods of heightened concentration, intense absorption, and feelings of accomplishment. She discussed emotional qualities of faculty work such as feeling unencumbered, acting decisively, and engaging in [an] activity worth pursuing for its own sake, which can arguably be likened to intrinsic motivation. Nevertheless, the higher education literature is sparse on this subject and more work is needed to further understand the connection between emotion and motivation.

Through a qualitative approach, the purpose of this chapter is to offer a perspective of faculty work that examines the role that emotions play in the academic life of fifteen underrepresented faculty members in science and engineering at a predominantly white institution (PWI). I utilize the conceptual framework of emotion management (Ashforth and Tomuik, 2000; Erickson and Ritter, 2001) to examine the influence of emotions on faculty work life. As such, I will focus the discussion on understanding the extent to which emotion management influences faculty motivation to engage in scholarly work within the sociocultural setting of a PWI. I begin with a brief discussion regarding the link between emotions and motivation, before providing a general understanding of the two constructs that form the basis of the emotion management framework: *emotional labor* and *emotion work*. Information on the recruitment of the participants and the qualitative methods used to gather and analyze data is presented before I discuss in detail the three themes that fall under the umbrella of emotion management resulted from the data analysis. I conclude the chapter with implications to administrators and institutional researchers and suggestions about potential means to help underrepresented faculty at PWIs manage their emotions with the ultimate goal to maintain their motivation and improve their productivity.

Theoretical Grounding

Linking Emotion and Motivation. Much has been written about the link between emotion and motivation (Bierema, 2001; Callahan and McCollum, 2002; Jarvis, 2006; Neumann, 2006). Deci (1996) argues that emotion and motivation can be examined through motivation theory; however, there are limitations in doing so. As he states, "The limitation concerns the complex interplay between emotion as an energizer of action and the role of cognitions in the mediation of emotion-motivated behavior" (p. 221). In other words, there are challenges associated with understanding how individuals cognitively reflect on an "event" or "stimulus" that causes them to feel an emotion, and the result of that cognitive process, that is, an emotion-motivated behavior. For example, if a faculty member of color overhears a colleague describing her or him as inept (the event or stimulus), then the manner in which that faculty member cognitively reflects on that "event" mediates how he or she is motivated to behave. The faculty member may immediately react with anger but, after taking some time to reflect (the cognitive process), realize that the comment was made in jest. The cognitive process mediates how an individual is motivated to react.

Emotion Management Framework. The process of managing one's emotions is "labor-intensive work; it is skilled; it is effort-intensive, and productive labor" (Steinberg and Figart, 1999, p. 9). It requires individuals to understand the context of their social environment, its behavioral norms, and the process of self-reflection. Emotion management, as utilized in this study, is premised on the idea that individuals have the ability to regulate their emotions. This conceptual framework consists of two constructs: (1) emotional labor and (2) emotion work.

Emotional Labor. Much of the research on managing emotions in the workplace is found in the business and management disciplines. Hochschild (1979, 1983) coined the term *emotional labor* and defined it as the act of creating or displaying socially desired behaviors. Emotional labor concerns itself with "the management of feelings to create *publicly* observable facial and bodily displays" (Hochschild, 1983, p. 7) that conform to particular sociocontextual norms, such as a college classroom or a faculty meeting. The foundation of emotional labor is grounded on the *relational* component of an occupation. Regardless of occupation, if one is required to continually interact with others and conform to display rules, then there is a likelihood that an individual will engage in emotional labor, and the manner in which we publicly express our emotions is linked to whether or not we are behaving authentically.

Authentic behavior is grounded on the notion that one possesses knowledge about the "self." Within the context of teaching, Palmer (1998) contends that self-knowledge is at the heart of authentic behavior. If individuals are not in touch with their personal beliefs and values, they may have difficulty expressing authentic behavior. Cranton and Carusseta (2004) argue, "To be able to express the genuine self people need to know who the self is" (p. 7). They build on this idea by asserting that authentic behavior expresses the veritable self within a social community. Put differently, when an individual behaves authentically, he or she displays consistency of values and behaviors in relationships with others. Difficult questions arise, however, in considering the idea of self-knowledge (Dirkx, 2006). Scholars maintain that critical self-reflection is needed to develop an understanding of self (Brookfield, 1995).

Inauthentic behavior is a notion developed by Hochschild (1979, 1983) through studying workers in service professions, for example, sales professionals, nurses, and teachers. She argued that particular expectations about the appropriate behaviors and emotions exist in service transactions and "give rise to feeling rules or norms that specify the range, intensity, durations, and object of emotions that should be experienced" (Ashforth and Humphrey, 1993, p. 89). For instance, customer service personnel are expected to be helpful and positive, nurses are expected to feel compassion and caring, and therapists are expected to be supportive and empathetic. Inauthentic behavior is grounded on the idea that individuals suppress their genuine feelings to comply with specific emotional and behavioral rules (Hochschild, 1983). When they are compelled to follow behavioral displays that are not in concert with their true emotions, this behavior is said to be inauthentic.

Inauthentic behavior can lead to both psychological and physical dysfunctions (Parkinson, 1991). For instance, Rutter and Fielding (1988) found that prison guards' need to suppress emotions was positively associated with stress and negatively associated with job satisfaction. One can argue that if faculty members feel the need to suppress their emotions to adapt to the socially constructed norms of the department, the professoriate, and the culture of academe, such suppression can cause psychological dysfunctions and affect their physical health over time. Ashforth and Humphrey (1993) propose that, "If emotional labor is inconsistent with a central, salient, and valued social and/or personal identity, it will lead to emotive dissonance and/or a loss of one's sense of authentic self" (p. 101). Said differently, if individuals are consistently working to suppress genuine emotions and behaviors that are incongruent with their values and identity, they risk losing their sense of self or authenticity.

Emotion Work. Emotion work serves as a second construct in the emotion management framework. Erickson and Ritter (2001) distinguish between emotional labor and emotion work by explaining that emotional labor concerns itself with the public display of emotions that are "performed in the workplace for a wage" (p. 146), whereas emotion work takes place in private and pertains to the psychological effects of emotional labor. Context differentiates emotional labor from emotion work (Erickson and Ritter, 2001), and the management of emotions represents the link between with the two.

Emotion work is defined as *the act of trying* to change one's emotion. It emphasizes the effort one makes to change his or her emotions (Hochschild, 1979). Moreover, emotion work does not focus on the outcome of one's attempt. Instead, "Failed acts of management still indicate what ideal formulations guide the effort ..." (Hochschild, 1979, p. 556). Emotion work requires personal reflection that results in an active attempt to change one's feelings (Hochschild, 1979) to mitigate the psychological effects of the feeling rules associated with his or her job. For example, emotion work can be characterized by phrases such as, "I'm going to focus on being positive" or "I need to stay calm and quiet at the faculty meeting." Whether or not the outcomes of such attempts are successful is irrelevant. The act of attempting to shape or trigger an emotion is what differentiates emotion work from emotional labor.

In summary, an individual's affective or displayed behavior serves as the basis from which to manage emotions. Interacting with colleagues requires individuals to display certain emotions as determined by "feeling rules" (Hochschild, 1979), which can be used interchangeably with "display

Table 5.1. Emotion Management Framework

Two Components	Emotion Management	
	Emotional Labor	Emotion Work
Distinctive characteristics	Occurs in public	Occurs in private
	Premised on interactions with others	Is a personal undertaking
	Behavior as a "performance" based on compliance with "feeling" rules	Concerns itself with the psychological consequences of performing behavior
	Individuals can display authentic behaviors	Individuals engage in a cognitive reflection process
	Individuals can also display inauthentic behaviors	Individuals work to mitigate psychological effects of emotional labor

rules" (Ekman, 1973; Rafaeli and Sutton, 1989). The act of conforming or attempting to conform to such rules (for example, "collegial" behavior) forms the basis of emotional labor (Ekman, 1973). On the other hand, the process of reflecting on one's affective behavior forms the foundation of emotion work. The extent to which individuals behave according to what they consider to be their true or genuine self can affect feelings associated with emotional exhaustion and job satisfaction (Abraham, 1998). To better illustrate how emotional labor and emotion work are distinctly different but related to one another, a comparison between the two concepts is made in Table 5.1.

Methods

Data for this chapter were drawn from a qualitative study that explored faculty motivation to engage in research activities utilizing the constructivist paradigm of naturalistic inquiry (Lincoln and Guba, 1985). Naturalistic inquiry is based on the assumption that knowledge exists within the meaning that is attached to the phenomenon under examination and allows for the co-construction of knowledge between myself, the researcher, and study participants (Guba and Lincoln, 1989). Data were collected through semistructured interviews lasting between fifty and ninety minutes. Semistructured interviews were chosen because of the fluid nature of the study, which allowed for variations in participants' responses and researcher probes (Patton, 2002). Interviews ranged in length from fifty to ninety minutes, with the majority lasting approximately sixty minutes. Subsequent communication took place either by e-mail or by telephone for purposes of seeking clarification of data and/or to probe for additional data that would allow for a more thorough analysis.

A total of fifteen faculty members in science and engineering fields, from a predominantly white research university, participated in this study. All interviews were audiotaped and subsequently transcribed for analysis. I selected participants through a purposeful sampling of 52 tenured and tenure-track underrepresented faculty members from a pool of a population of 393 faculty in STEM (science, technology, engineering, and mathematics) disciplines. Potential participants were identified using publicly available data on the university's website. E-mail invitations were sent to faculty members in the Biological Sciences, Computer Sciences, Engineering, and Mathematics departments, of which I received 21 responses. Scheduling conflicts allowed for only 15 of the 21 respondents to be interviewed. Faculty members were evenly distributed by rank: 5 assistant, 5 associate, and 5 full professors. With regard to race and ethnicity, 13 identified as Latino, 1 as black, and 1 did not identify himself as belonging to any ethnic group, although he acknowledged his Latino ancestry.

The study site was chosen primarily for two reasons. First, the institution is a member of the Association of American Universities, a sixty-two-member association of the top research universities in the United States and Canada. Second, many of the university's science and engineering programs consistently rank among the top fifteen programs at U.S. public universities. Most recently, the College of Engineering was ranked among the top ten in the 2010 *U.S. News & World Report*.

Data were initially coded based on the various concepts and experiences participants discussed. I analyzed initial codes to develop categories that spoke to broader topical areas and used the constant comparative method during data analysis (Glaser and Strauss, 1967; Strauss and Corbin, 1998). In other words, interview data were continuously analyzed and compared to one another, and categories were integrated in numerous ways so as to offer multiple interpretations that allowed for "thick description." After grouping data by category, I focused my analysis on refining each category before "reassembling" data into broad themes (Strauss and Corbin, 1998).

I ensured credibility and trustworthiness (Guba and Lincoln, 1989) by reviewing multiple data sources, evaluating data across interviews, and rechecking data with participants during and after the interview period. This triangulation process allowed me to "examine conclusions (assertions, claims, etc.) from more than one vantage point" (Schwandt, 2001, p. 257) and to ensure that findings were "worth paying attention to" (Guba and Lincoln, 1989, p. 290). Moreover, this reassured that data were not misread or misinterpreted. Other data sources used during the triangulation process included publicly available demographic information about students and faculty; information gathered from department, college, and university websites; and university reports from the university's office of assessment and office of admissions.

NEW DIRECTIONS FOR INSTITUTIONAL RESEARCH • DOI: 10.1002/ir

Findings

Study findings demonstrate how participants managed emotions associated with faculty employment at a predominantly white institution in fields in which minorities are grossly underrepresented, for example, science and engineering. While space limitations do not allow for a detailed presentation of the findings, I offer readers a broad overview of how faculty participants utilized the two constructs of emotion management—emotional labor and emotion work—to remain motivated to engage in their work. I present three themes that delineate participants' emotional challenges and coping mechanisms they used when engaging in inauthentic and authentic behaviors to manage their emotions: (1) complying with others, (2) remaining silent, and (3) mental preparation and resistance.

Complying with Others. Participants consistently expressed the need to follow or comply with "suggestions" offered by individuals in positions of authority, regardless of whether these propositions were in their best interest. A tenured participant explained, "A lot of university officials have hired [senior] administrators that are not scientists or professors, and then you feel like you have to do whatever they say even though they really don't understand your field." Data also revealed that "compliance" was most prevalent during the pretenure years. An associate professor in engineering recalled how as an assistant professor he was asked by his department head to coauthor grant proposals, "The only thing my department head, my then department head, the only thing he wanted was to exploit me to get money as opposed to help me develop my career."

An associate professor in biological sciences offered a similar example:

> My department head very much encouraged me to get involved with the creation of a huge national center in genomics and biogenomics, and stuff like that. And that sucked away three years of my assistant professorship that was basically washed down the drain because in the end, the grant didn't get funded. And that was a huge waste of my time that put my tenure in danger.

Using a different example, an assistant professor understood the importance of attending a professional conference his department head valued. He made efforts to comply with this implicit responsibility:

> Now there are certain things that you should do. ... For instance, we have the American Association for Engineering Education that [my department head] is a big proponent of, and one of the things I was told was "it's a good idea to attend this conference."

He explained that he has "submitted a paper to that conference every year because that's his [department head's] thing, and if you get involved with it, he views it favorably. So that's probably the only thing that I feel like that they kind of push you to do. . . ." Finally, a senior professor of biology summed up the emotional labor associated with being an untenured faculty member and how faculty culture compels one to comply with the "feeling rules" of academe:

> I think being an assistant professor is unnecessarily difficult and is putting stress and tension on the family, and personal life. It's like "if you don't [follow] these sets of rules, I won't accept you to be part of my club," and then you have to follow the fools hoping and praying that they are going to accept you to the club, right?

Remaining Silent. Many participants spoke about incidents regarding racism, ethnocentrism, homophobia, and their perceived inability to speak out because of the institution's display rules. For example, a faculty member described an incident that occurred while he was being evaluated for promotion to full professor. Senior faculty members pulled him into an office and said to him, "All the janitorial [staff] are Hispanic. You should be one of those," they were commenting. "White Anglo-Saxons were telling me this in this office that I was a nobody that I shouldn't be here." He explained how he remained collegial in his interactions with those colleagues, regardless of their perceptions and behaviors, and was promoted to full professor by year's end.

Participants as a whole commented that the university climate was unwelcoming to faculty of color. A respondent provided examples of how some white faculty members created an unfriendly environment for underrepresented faculty. "It's the way people look at you. The way they consider your comments, the importance of your opinions, [and] the jokes that are made around you."

At least four of the participants commented on how difficult the climate was for women of color in science and engineering. A full professor described a conversation he heard with a white individual and a Hispanic female engineering professor, and how she failed to realize the "compliments" she made to the professor were actually degrading.

> You need to talk to Hispanic women in science and you will see an amazing world ... these women have experienced certain things, you know. People telling them things like "Oh my God" after they finished their talk. "Oh, you're so bright. You know I only thought about Hispanic people as lazy and ignorant, but you have changed the way I see them now."

Faculty described other instances that required them to keep their emotions in check when junior and senior faculty members interacted with one another. A biological science professor recalled the difficulties his department had in creating a "community of scholars":

NEW DIRECTIONS FOR INSTITUTIONAL RESEARCH • DOI: 10.1002/ir

You know [all the faculty], on Fridays, try to have discussions about science. And in my opinion, those things turned from being opportunities where, as scientists, we could interact together into quizzes that the senior faculty would give to the junior faculty. Like, "What?!?" I mean I am like, "So what are you doing to me? You are quizzing me as opposed to, you know? Is that the way you are helping me?"

The stress associated with having to remain silent and go along with the "quiz game" took a psychological toll on that faculty member. An assistant professor commented, "It affects your productivity, of course. . . . If you don't feel like the [department] supports you fully, you don't want to work for that institution fully either."

Mental Preparation and Resistance. Findings within this theme revealed how participants engaged in emotion work to actively manage their emotions by mentally preparing themselves to adapt to the challenging university climate and the culture of the professoriate. Proactive actions and positive reflection seemed to be a recurring theme among participants, which reflects how often they intentionally reflected on behaviors that could lead to positive emotional outcomes. One participant, for instance, discussed how he consciously prepared himself for a potential backlash from some faculty during his bid for tenure. His reflection process was to focus on the positive outcome (tenure) rather than on focusing on perfection. "I understood that from the very beginning that I was never going to [unanimously] satisfy the tenure and promotion committee. There was always going to be somebody who was going to be dissatisfied. . . ." By focusing on the broader picture (being granted tenure) and preparing himself for the possibility that some of his colleagues would not view him as worthy of promotion and tenure, he successfully managed his emotions so as not to allow negative characterizations to affect his motivation to engage in scholarly activities. He added, "I have seen careers destroyed of young faculty because of one negative vote, it has destroyed them . . . destroyed their perception, their perceptions of themselves, that they are worthless, that all of a sudden their work is not good."

At least six participants used a different technique to engage in thinking about ways to redirect their negative feelings in a constructive manner. An associate professor described his initial feeling about the institutional culture and demonstrated the process he used to manage his emotions.

Here, I told you, it felt like I came back to the U.S. in the 50s, so people don't know anything [about diversity], I mean a lot of stereotypes. You hear things that you would never hear anywhere else. I like that because I have teaching moments for me. I have had students that, because they have several interactions with me, they have changed their ways about how they think about certain things.

He explained that his job situation "makes me extremely happy. So for me, because I have that mind-set, it's a perfect place to be."

In addition to mental preparedness, one participant described how he consistently elicited emotions related to activism to cope with an institutional climate unwelcoming of diversity. He explained that an inherent characteristic of his persona was his resilient attitude, which has enabled him to flourish in an environment that is less than friendly to minorities. "I have always been considered an activist, involved in activism and minority issues and stuff. ... I have a fighter spirit because I have always been associated with activism." He suggested that other minority faculty would benefit from evoking their "fighter spirit" because, as he put it, "If you are not of the activist mind, you will leave [this university]. You will not think this place is a place that respects you." By directing his emotions in such a way, he was able to emotionally cope with the institutional culture without hindering his productivity. Other faculty described the importance of evoking proactive behaviors that led to positive outlooks as a way to ensure that they would be able to focus on their work responsibilities: "You get to your office, there are many things in your head bothering you ... and so working on those issues in advance and trying to solve them instead of letting them accumulate and get worse [is a form of mental preparation]".

Discussion

I began this chapter by arguing that emotions can influence motivation and pointed to extant literature in various disciplines as a place of reference. What has yet to be examined is the specific connection between emotion management and faculty motivation. Scholars have argued that the degree to which individuals feel in control of their work life influences their intrinsic motivation (Deci and Ryan, 1985) and predicts their psychological health (Kohn and Schooler, 1983; Mirowsky and Ross, 1989). The more in control one feels, the fewer feelings of burnout and inauthenticity (Bulan, Erickson, and Wharton, 1997; Erickson and Wharton 1997), as well as an increase in motivation (Deci and Ryan, 1985). Similarly, if individuals feel controlled by their work or environment, then they are likely to feel less intrinsically motivated. For example, the theme "Remaining Silent" indicates how inauthentic behavior can restrict one's autonomy because an individual is compelled to behave inauthentically so as to conform to the feeling rules of academe. Remaining silent may take a harder toll on underrepresented faculty when derogatory remarks are made about them, their abilities, or other minority faculty. Underrepresented faculty may feel the need to suppress feelings of anger in order to conform to the display rules, thus infringing on their ability to determine their own behavior and hindering the development of intrinsic motivation. Consequently, "hiding one's feelings of anger may harm well-being because it is a further indicator of one's relatively disadvantaged status or lack of control over the emotion management process" (Erickson and Ritter, 2001, p. 151). Individuals that feel their autonomy is restricted are more likely to feel less motivated.

Emotion work in the form of preemptive reflection contributes to individuals' ability to maintain their authenticity. The notion of the authenticity is grounded on one's ability *to know* who the genuine "self" is (Cranton and Carusseta, 2004). The danger is that it is possible for some faculty to lose the ability to locate their authenticity by consistently having to behave inauthentically during their probationary period, which typically lasts between five and seven years. After they are awarded tenure, they may no longer have a clear sense of what they consider to be their authentic self, which can lead to behaviors that inhibit intrinsic motivation. Displaying professional behavior is not uncommon in the workplace, nor is it always considered to be inauthentic. Yet problems arise when there is internal conflict (internal to the individual) about one's ability to know whether he or she is behaving authentically, thus negatively influencing motivation.

The manner in which emotions are managed within the context of the professoriate is linked to the feeling rules of higher education, in this case the norms that specify how and to what degree emotions are to be publicly experienced and displayed by faculty members, and the implicit rules to which faculty must comply to be promoted and/or tenured. Emotion management in higher education differs from other professional contexts partially because of the tenure and promotion system. Tenure is unique to the professoriate, and essentially does not exist outside the confines of colleges and universities. Thus, emotion management for faculty in tenure-track/tenured positions arguably differs greatly from individuals in other professions. As the data show, emotional labor for participants centered on compliance and silence, two categories that do not vary greatly from the emotional labor experienced by service workers (Hochschild, 1979, 1983; Tschan, Rochat, and Zapf, 2005). I argue, however, that the stakes are higher for faculty who do not comply with the display rules of the professoriate; that is, their careers are jeopardized. In relative terms, emotional labor may impose a greater toll on faculty and may require a greater amount of emotion work. Additional empirical research is needed to determine whether this assertion is accurate. What the data do show is that inauthentic behavior plays a large role in the work lives of faculty, most often on assistant and associate professors, and the tenure system may arguably cause psychological and physical damage to professors. This is not to say that tenure should be eliminated. Rather, institutions ought to consider how their tenure and promotion systems can be altered in ways to make the process less psychologically stressful for their faculty.

This study has wide-ranging implications for university administrators, institutional researchers, and other policymaking bodies. On a foundational level, stakeholders ought to explicitly acknowledge that faculty members experience positive and negative emotions as a result of their work lives, and these emotions can influence their motivation. The behavioral norms of academe make it difficult to identify faculty who may be in need of emotional support. It may be prudent for administrators and senior faculty to be proactive in developing a healthy psychological environment that does not cause additional stress to faculty members. All faculty members, including those seeking promotion through the ranks, are under a tremendous amount of stress. Institutional effort to ensure that their work environment is as stress-free as possible is a starting point that can foment intrinsic motivation.

The long-term goals ought to focus on shifting the cultural norms of the professoriate. The behavioral norms of academe are arguably rigid and confining. In many cases, they do not allow for behavioral missteps, such as losing control of one's emotions during a faculty meeting. Such behavior ought not determine how faculty members are perceived (hostile or noncollegial), for the remainder of their probationary or prepromotion period. Through conducting institutional research on faculty emotions, administrators at all levels can begin to foster an academic culture that focuses on empathy and compassion among faculty members, especially between pretenured and senior faculty members. Ensuring that there are "spaces" where faculty can behave authentically is significant to their psychological welfare. Creating spaces may simply mean sponsoring opportunities for faculty to interact socially with other faculty outside their departments or colleges. They can also take place within the confines of a trustworthy faculty mentoring relationship.

Institutional researchers may need to collect qualitative data through occasionally surveying or interviewing faculty members on their work-related emotional status, motivation, and satisfaction. Information on faculty psychological welfare can guide deans, department heads, and campus administrators in their management and policymaking. Also, faculty development professionals can take advantage of the information and offer workshops on how faculty can maintain motivation through the use of emotion management techniques. Such efforts would communicate to faculty that the university as a whole, along with deans and department heads, is mindful of the emotional stress that faculty face. Findings from this study imply that that institutional culture may play a role in the degree to which faculty members will engage in emotional labor. Given that the university studied here is predominantly white with regard to faculty and students and has a reputation for being unfriendly to underrepresented minorities, it should not be surprising to find that underrepresented faculty may need to engage in a high level of emotional labor. Nevertheless, the broad goal of this chapter is to *acknowledge* the emotional stress that faculty must manage and assist them in addressing how to manage such stress. In the long run, such efforts may contribute to increased motivation, satisfaction, retention, and productivity of faculty members.

NEW DIRECTIONS FOR INSTITUTIONAL RESEARCH • DOI: 10.1002/ir

References

Abraham, R. "Emotional Dissonance in Organizations: Antecedents, Consequences, and Moderators." *Genetic, Social, and Gender Psychology Monographs*, 1998, *124*, 229–246.

Ashforth, B. E., and Humphrey, R. H. "Emotional Labor in Service Roles: The Influence of Identity." *Academy of Management Review*, 1993, *18*(1), 88–115.

Ashforth, B. E., and Tomuik, M. A. "Emotional Labour and Authenticity: Views from Service Agents." In S. Fineman (ed.), *Emotion in Organizations* (2nd ed.). Thousand Oaks, Calif.: Sage, 2000.

Bierema, L. "Adult Learning in the Workplace: Emotion Work or Emotion Learning?" In J. M. Dirkx (ed.), *The New Update on Adult Learning Theory.* New Directions for Adult and Continuing Education, *Vol. 89.* San Francisco: Jossey-Bass, 2001.

Brookfield, S. D. *Becoming a Critically Reflective Teacher.* San Francisco: Jossey-Bass, 1995.

Bulan, H. F., Erickson, R. J., and Wharton, A. S. "Doing for Others on the Job: The Affective Requirements of Service Work, Gender, and Emotional Well-Being." *Social Problems*, 1997, *44*, 701–723.

Callahan, J. L., and McCollum, E. E. "Conceptualization of Emotion Research in Organizational Contexts." *Advances in Developing Human Resources*, 2002, *4*(1), 4–21.

Cranton, P. and Carusseta, E. "Perspectives on Authenticity in Teaching." *Adult Education Quarterly*, 2004, *55*(1), 5–22.

Deci, E. L. "Making Room for Self-Regulation: Some Thoughts on the Link Between Emotion and Motivation." *Psychological Inquiry*, 1996, *7*(3), 220–223.

Deci, E. L., and Ryan, R. M. *Intrinsic Motivation and Self-Determination in Human Behavior.* New York: Plenum, 1985.

Dirkx, J. "Engaging Emotions in Adult Learning: A Jungian Perspective on Emotion and Transformative Learning." *New Directions for Adult and Continuing Education*, 2006, *109*, 15–26. San Francisco: Jossey-Bass.

Ekman, P. "Cross-Cultural Studies of Facial Expression." In P. Ekman (ed.), *Darwin and Facial Expression: A Century of Research.* New York: Academic Press, 1973.

Erickson, R. J., and Ritter, C. "Emotional Labor, Burnout, and Inauthenticity: Does Gender Matter?" *Social Psychology Quarterly*, 2001, *64*(2), 146–163.

Erickson, R. J., and Wharton, A. S. "Inauthenticity and Depression: Assessing the Consequences of Interactive Service Work." *Work and Occupations*, 1997, *24*(2), 188–213.

Glaser, B. G., and Strauss, A. L. *The Discovery of Grounded Theory: Strategies for Qualitative Research.* Chicago: Aldine, 1967.

Guba, E., and Lincoln, Y. *Fourth Generation Evaluation.* Newbury Park, Calif.: Sage, 1989.

Hochschild, A. R. "Emotion Work, Feeling Rules, and Social Structure." *American Journal of Sociology*, 1979, *85*, 551–575.

Hochschild, A. R. *The Managed Heart: Commercialization of Human Feelings.* Berkeley: University of California Press, 1983.

Jarvis, P. *Toward a Comprehensive Theory of Human Learning.* London: Routledge, 2006.

Kohn, M. L., and Schooler, C. *Work and Personality.* Norwood, N.J.: Ablex, 1983.

Lincoln, Y. S., and Guba, E. G. *Naturalistic Inquiry.* Newberry Park, Calif.: Sage, 1985.

Mirowsky, J., and Ross, C. E. *Social Causes of Psychological Distress.* New York: Aldine, 1989.

Neumann, A. "Professing Passion: Emotion in Scholarship of Professors at Research Universities." *American Educational Research Journal*, 2006, *43*(3), 381–424.

Palmer, P. *The Courage to Teach: Exploring the Inner Landscape of a Teacher's Life.* San Francisco: Jossey-Bass, 1998.

Parkinson, B. "Emotional Stylists: Strategies of Expressive Management Among Trainee Hairdressers." *Cognition and Emotion*, 1991, 5, 419–434.

Patton, M. Q. *Qualitative Research and Evaluation Methods* (3rd ed.). Thousand Oaks, Calif.: Sage, 2002.

Rafaeli, A., and Sutton, R. I. "The Expression of Emotion in Organizational Life." In L. L. Cummings and B. M. Staw (eds.), *Research in Organizational Behavior*, Vol. 11. Greenwich, Conn.: JAI Press, 1989.

Rutter, D. R., and Fielding, P. J. "Sources of Occupational Stress: An Examination of British Prison Officers." *Work & Stress*, 1988, 2(4), 291–299.

Schwandt, T. A. *Dictionary of Qualitative Inquiry* (2nd ed.). Thousand Oaks, Calif.: Sage, 2001.

Smith, E., and Witt, S. L. "A Comparative Study of Occupational Stress Among African Americans and White University Faculty: A Research Note." *Research in Higher Education*, 1993, 34(2), 229–241.

Steinberg, R. J., and Figart, D. M. "Emotional Labor Since *The Managed Heart*." *Annals of the American Academy of Political and Social Science*, 1999, 561, 8–26.

Strauss, A., and Corbin, J. *Basics of Qualitative Research: Techniques and Procedures for Developing Grounded Theory* (2nd ed.). Thousand Oaks, Calif.: Sage, 1998.

Tschan, F., Rochat, S., and Zapf, D. "It's Not Only Clients: Studying Emotion Work With Clients and Co-workers With an Event-Sampling Approach." *Journal of Occupational and Organizational Psychology*, 2005, 78, 195–220.

VICENTE M. LECHUGA is associate professor of higher education administration at Texas A&M University.

NEW DIRECTIONS FOR INSTITUTIONAL RESEARCH • DOI: 10.1002/ir

6

Four themes that have emerged from the previous chapters are discussed; changes and improvements are suggested for future data collection and institutional research on faculty diversity.

Lessons from the Past and Directions for the Future

Yonghong Jade Xu

There is a steady line of research to understand faculty diversity and its impact on the work life quality of faculty and learning outcomes of students in the U.S. higher education systems. What makes this volume unique is that, rather than treating diversity as a static and simplistic concept, the chapter authors presented information to show the progressing diversification of faculty population, as defined by factors including gender, race, national origin, job status, and academic disciplines. In this chapter, I synthesize the previous five chapters and discuss the four themes that have emerged.

The Multilayer Diversity of Faculty Population

Faculty diversity can no longer be simply defined by percentage distributions by gender and racial/ethnic groups. As demonstrated in the previous chapters, the attributes of the academic work environment, which segment faculty by institutional types, academic disciplines, rank and tenure systems, job status (full time versus part time), result in individuals from different subgroups having distinct experiences. Such diversity is further complicated by the social and cultural identity maintained by faculty of different gender, nationality, and racial/ethnic background. A faculty population of increasing diversity means that, when examining the professional experience of postsecondary faculty, we need to be sensitive to subgroup differences, and especially mindful about the underrepresented groups' experiences. Also, with evidence showing that how a faculty member interprets the work environment has a direct impact on one's teaching and research productivity, institutional research (IR) officers are expected to do more than summarize the campus diversity efforts with percentage distribution of faculty by gender and race. In order to move the diversity agenda forward and create an inclusive campus climate, institutional researchers need to (1) create a more rigorous and systematic data system to collect and manage diverse faculty information; (2) constantly remind campus administrators and policymakers of the impact of faculty work conditions on the educational outcomes of the institution, including student performance and graduation rate; and (3) monitor the changing profile of faculty population, and provide in-depth knowledge of their work conditions, motivation, and other perspectives of the professional experience.

Progressive Diversification of Faculty Population

In Chapters 1, 2, and 3, the authors used empirical data to show that faculty diversity, from multiple perspectives, has progressed over time. For example, in Chapter 1, Smith, Tovar, and García observed substantial differences in the percentage growth between 1993 and 2009 of faculty by racial/ethnic group: "White faculty grew by 20 percent (with women growing 56 percent), blacks by 58 percent (women by 80 percent), Latinos by 132 percent (women by 185 percent), AA/PI by 140 percent (women by 260 percent), AI/AN by 85 percent (women by 131 percent), and [nonresident aliens] by 188 percent (women 333 percent)." These increases also serve as a clear indication that "women faculty grew substantially faster across all racial groups and within institutional types than men."

In Chapter 2, Kim, Twombly, and Wolf-Wendel concurred with the authors of Chapter 1 on the growing presence of international faculty in U.S. higher education institutions, and brought to our attention that "the proportional representation of foreign-born faculty easily surpasses that of domestic underrepresented racial/ethnic groups." Their data also revealed significant differences in the distribution of international faculty across academic disciplines: "The percentage distributions of international faculty range from 8.9 percent in education to 42.6 percent in engineering" and, as a minority group, they "concentrated in the natural science and engineering fields . . . (35 percent of faculty in engineering and 39 percent in computer science)."

In Chapter 3, Kezar and Maxey brought to focus the increasing number of non-tenure-track faculty, and use the Integrated Postsecondary Education Data System (IPEDS) 2007 data to show that 66 percent of all faculty appointments are made off the tenure track and approximately 47 percent of all faculty appointments made were part-time positions.

With the striking changes in the makeup of faculty population, institutional researchers need to be mindful of examining faculty diversity and how it has changed over time. Actively tracking *changes* over time is important in order to provide enlightening information about the professional life of faculty on campus. Here, *changes* not only present themselves as numerical fluctuations of some static groups, but as a developing definition of "diversity" itself. For instance, several decades ago, rarely was there any mention of international or nonresident alien faculty in diversity research, and part-time faculty was thought to be an isolated phenomenon in two-year institutions. Now international and non-tenure-track faculty contribute to the diversity of the professoriate across institutional types. As discussed in the previous chapters, changes and diversification of faculty population impact the work experience of faculty as well as the college experience of students. Institutional data collection and research need to be sensitive to such changes and provide administrators and stakeholders with up-to-date knowledge to guide their diversity efforts and policies.

Importance of Data Collection on Higher Education Faculty

We all understand that reliable data sources and accurate data collection are the basic requirements for ensuring the trustworthiness of the research. Reliable and systematic data collection on non-tenure-track faculty dominated the discussion in Chapter 3. The same chapter also serves as a reminder that data collection on the general faculty population remains a challenge, especially after the discontinuation of the National Study of Postsecondary Faculty (NSOPF). Although sample based, the NSOPF data provide systematic and comprehensive inquiry about faculty productivity and professional experiences in the U.S. higher education system. With multiple implementations of consistent survey questions, the data may have been the only source at the national level that enabled researchers to investigate the changes in faculty experience overtime, as illustrated in Chapters 1, 2, and 4.

In the post-NSOPF era, one of the major tasks for institutional researchers is to be creative and collaborative in our data collection effort. With comfort, we learn that there are organizations working to collect faculty data. For instance, in Chapter 3, Kezar and Maxey introduced the Coalition on the Academic Workforce (CAW) and New Faculty Majority (NFM) and their effort to collect data on non-tenure-track faculty. The Collaborative on Academic Careers in Higher Education (COACHE) at the Harvard Graduate School of Education has recruited more than 200 colleges and universities to collect data on job satisfaction of both pretenure and tenured faculty. The Higher Education Research Institute (HERI) at the University of California Los Angeles also operates a faculty survey, the focus of which is to measure faculty's perspectives on instruction-related issues and how they impact students' experience. However, two disadvantages are common among these institution-sponsored survey programs. First is the lack of systematic sampling in the data collection process due to their reliance on members to volunteer faculty data. The self-selection nature sets the surveys apart from NSOPF, which used stratified sampling procedures to select nationally representative samples of postsecondary faculty from two- and four-year public and nonprofit private institutions, and puts in question the generalizability of findings of the studies using these survey data. Second, concerned with financial costs and low response rates to lengthy questionnaires, institution-sponsored surveys focus their questions on restricted aspects of faculty work experience. As a result of the lack of comprehensiveness, these surveys are unable to fill the void left by NSOPF, in particular for researchers who are interested in studying how diversity of the faculty population is related to different aspects of their professional experiences.

With some naïveté, I propose two possible approaches for future data collection on higher education faculty. First, institutional researchers, through connections at professional organizations such as the Association for Institutional Research (AIR), may organize data collection on faculty in a collaborative fashion. Consulting with researchers and faculty members who have expertise on faculty issues, a software development company can be hired to design and implement a data management system that runs on a Windows platform. The cost would be reasonable to digest when shared by member institutions. Researchers will collect faculty data within their institutions on a regular basis, and the shared system will allow data merging and centralized management following the decentralized data collection. This volunteer approach is not ideal for collecting data from the faculty population or from a representative sample, but it makes it feasible to gather more comprehensive information on faculty, including their demographics, job status, productivity, and, if surveys are used, both quantitative and qualitative data on their perception of the academic work environment and other related professional experiences.

The second approach is to request a federal agency, such as the National Center for Education Statistics (NCES), to resume their data collection on postsecondary faculty. The nationally representative samples, the multicycle implementations, and the comprehensiveness of the survey questions are difficult to match without supports at the federal level. However, to take this approach, we first need to learn lessons from the discontinuation of NSOPF—it is said that this project was discontinued by the Department of Education during the recent financial crisis, mainly due to the lack of evidence to persuade the Education Committee of the Congress that the surveys of postsecondary faculty had produced meaningful impacts on the nation's educational outcomes. The fund originally intended for NSOPF is now used to conduct postsecondary education transcript studies (PETS) as part of the longitudinal studies of students. It is discouraging to realize that, after decades of inquiries and efforts of generations of scholars and researchers, our research findings failed to convince the public, the stakeholders, and policymakers that

> [Faculty] directly affect the quality of education in postsecondary institutions. Faculty are the pivotal resource around which the process and outcomes of postsecondary education revolve. They often determine curriculum content, student performance standards, and the quality of students' preparation for careers. Faculty members perform research and development work upon which this nation's technological and economic advancement depends. (National Center for Education Statistics, n.d.).

How much impact can we expect the studies of faculty diversity to have on institutional and public policymaking if the professional well-being of faculty, the primary production force of higher education, is ignored at the national level? Given the importance of data collection in producing scholarly studies and institutional research, actions ought to be taken to explore the possibility of reinstating NSOPF.

Flexibility with Both Qualitative and Quantitative Research Methodologies

To date, the majority of information handled by the IR offices on college and university campuses is numeric, or quantitative, in nature. Quantitative data may be sufficient to outline the general trends and identify major differences, but they cannot provide in-depth knowledge of the phenomena that we encounter. In both Chapters 2 and 3, the authors called for qualitative data collection by institutional researchers in order to gain a better understanding of the work experience of international faculty and non-tenure-track faculty members. In Chapter 5, a qualitative study of the underrepresented faculty members in STEM (science, technology, engineering, and mathematics) disciplines provided us rich information and profound understanding of the role that emotions played in their academic life. The realization of the value in qualitative information suggests that institutional researchers shall collect both quantitative and qualitative data when feasible and have flexibility in terms of choosing the appropriate research methodology for the research questions at hand.

In order to gather reliable qualitative data, it is necessary to have well-developed instruments (e.g., surveys and interview questionnaires). Annual data collection would be efficient with online electronic survey tools that can spare IR officers from the burden of laborious data entry. In addition, online surveys allow versatile design features that present different questions to diverse faculty groups, so that questions can be tailored specifically for non-tenure-track faculty members, international faculty members, and other underrepresented members. It is always a good

NEW DIRECTIONS FOR INSTITUTIONAL RESEARCH • DOI: 10.1002/ir

strategy to collaborate with other organizations on campus (for example, faculty senate) to ensure major areas of concern are covered for various subgroups and avoid faculty fatigue of repetitive surveying.

With the volume, I hope institutional researchers' appreciation of diverse faculty issues can be heightened. The growing international competition for talented faculty members should give us the sense of urgency to care for the professional well-being of higher education faculty. Effective strategies to attract and retain quality faculty members would not be possible without an accurate understanding of the needs of our faculty with respect to their motivation, performance, and satisfaction that, as demonstrated by the chapter authors, can be dramatically different based on their diverse backgrounds.

Reference

National Center for Education Statistics. "National Study of Postsecondary Faculty: Overview." n.d. National Center for Educational Statistics. Retrieved January 21, 2012, from http://nces.ed.gov/surveys/nsopf/.

YONGHONG JADE XU is an associate professor of educational research at the University of Memphis.

NEW DIRECTIONS FOR INSTITUTIONAL RESEARCH • DOI: 10.1002/ir

INDEX

presence of women in STEM, women continue to leave at critical junctures in STEM training and careers at a higher rate than men. This volume of *New Directions for Institutional Research* takes a comprehensive look at the status of women in STEM and considers related factors, theoretical perspectives, and innovative tools that have the potential to help scholars understand, study, and improve the experiences of women in STEM fields.
ISBN: 978-1-1182-9769-8

IR 151   **Using Mixed-Methods Approaches to Study Intersectionality in Higher Education**
Kimberly A. Griffin, Samuel D. Museus
This volume of *New Directions for Institutional Research* focuses on using mixed-methods approaches and intersectionality frameworks in higher education research. The authors draw on intersectionality as a foundational theory for framing questions and interpreting results and discuss the importance of using a variety of methods to get useful, deep, honest answers from college faculty and students. They provide several examples of how such broad perspectives enhance the quality of scholarly and institutional research on faculty experiences and relationships, the challenges faced by faculty of color, college access and equity, privilege in higher education, campus climate research and assessment, and multiracial college students' experiences.
ISBN: 978-1-1181-7347-3

IR 150   **Validity and Limitations of College Student Self-Report Data**
Serge Herzog, Nicholas A. Bowman
Higher education administrators, institutional researchers (IR), and scholars rely heavily on the survey responses of college students, not least to meet mounting accountability pressures to document student learning and institutional effectiveness. However, research on the accuracy of students' self-reported learning, development, and experiences is quite limited. To address this critical issue, *Validity and Limitations of College Student Self-Report Data* provides seven empirical studies that examine the validity, use, and interpretation of such data, with an emphasis on student self-reported gains. The chapters are written by leading scholars in the field of college student self-reports, and they provide IR practitioners several analytical frameworks to gauge the accuracy of student survey data. The cumulative findings from this volume suggest that self-reported gains exhibit some significant biases, and they often do not constitute an adequate proxy for longitudinal measures of learning and development. Still, student self-reports offer important subjective impressions about learning and affective development that may complement direct measures of outcomes, together yielding a more comprehensive picture of the college experience.
ISBN: 978-1-1181-3416-0

IR 149   **Assessing Complex General Education Student Learning Outcomes**
Jeremy D. Penn
One of the greatest challenges in assessing student learning in general education programs is addressing the tension between selecting easy-to-measure learning outcomes that have little value or bearing on our institutions' goals and selecting meaningful and substantial learning outcomes that are complex and difficult to assess. Many institutions that have recently replaced their cafeteria-style general education programs with general education programs that focus on complex student learning outcomes find themselves at a loss in attempting to gather evidence on student achievement of these outcomes for internal improvement and external accountability purposes.

This volume of *New Directions for Institutional Research* makes a compelling case that institutions can and should be assessing consequential, complex general education student learning outcomes. It also gives faculty members and assessment leaders the tools and resources to take ownership of this important work. Part One of this volume provides an argument for why we should be assessing general education and describes a framework, based on a rigorous psychological research approach, for engaging in assessment. The six chapters in Part Two show how this work can be (and is being) done for six important learning outcomes: critical thinking, quantitative reasoning, teamwork, intercultural competence, civic knowledge and engagement, and integrative learning. The volume closes with recommendations on needed innovations in general education assessment and presents a research agenda for future work.
ISBN: 978-1-1180-9133-3

IR 148   **Students of Color in STEM**
Shaun R. Harper, Christopher B. Newman
Why are some racial minorities so underrepresented as degree candidates in science, technology, engineering, and mathematics (STEM)? Why are they so underprepared for college-level math and science courses? Why are their grades and other achievement indicators disproportionately lower than their white counterparts? Why do so many of them change their majors to non-STEM fields? And why do so few pursue graduate degrees in STEM? These five questions are continuously recycled in the study of students of color in STEM. Offered in this volume of *New Directions for Institutional Research* are new research ideas and frameworks that have emerged from recent studies of minorities in STEM fields across a wide array of institution types: large research universities, community colleges, minority-serving institutions, and others. The chapter authors counterbalance examinations of student underperformance and racial disparities in STEM with insights into the study of factors that enable minority student success.
ISBN: 978-1-1180-1402-8

IR 147   **System Offices for Community College Institutional Research**
Willard C. Hom
This volume of *New Directions for Institutional Research* examines a professional niche that tends to operate with a low profile while playing a major role in state policies—the system office for community college institutional research. As states, regions, and the federal government seek ways to evaluate and improve the performance of community colleges, this office has grown in importance. The chapter authors, all institutional researchers in this area, draw a timely state-of-the-niche portrait by showing how this office varies across states, how it varies from other institutional research offices within states, and the implications its history and prospects have for the future. This volume will be particularly useful for those who deal with higher education policy at the state, regional, or federal level; on-campus institutional researchers; and individuals who currently work in or with these system offices.
ISBN: 978-04709-39543

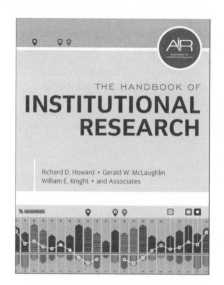

The Handbook of Institutional Research

Richard D. Howard,
Gerald W. McLaughlin,
William E. Knight,
and Associates

ISBN 978-0-470-60953-8
Hardcover | 768 pages

Institutional research is more relevant today than ever before as growing pressures for improved student learning and increased institutional accountability motivate higher education to effectively use ever-expanding data and information resources.

As the most current and comprehensive volume on the topic, the *Handbook* describes the fundamental knowledge, techniques, and strategies that define institutional research. The book contains an overview of the profession and its history, examines how institutional research supports executive and academic leadership and governance, and discusses the varied ways data from federal, state, and campus sources are used by research professionals.

Sponsored by the Association for Institutional Research, and with contributions from leading experts in the field, this important resource reviews the analytic tools, techniques and methodologies used by institutional researchers in their professional practice and covers a wide range of topics such as: conducting of institutional research; statistical applications; comparative analyses; quality control systems; measuring student, faculty, and staff opinions; and management activities designed to improve organizational effectiveness.